Help Your Child With

Reading

Nicky Solomon

The right of the
University of Cambridge
to print and sell
all manner of books
was granted by
Henry VIII in 1534.
The University has printed
and published continuously
since 1584.

Cambridge University Press

Cambridge

New York   Port Chester

Melbourne   Sydney

Published by the Press Syndicate of the University of Cambridge
The Pitt Building, Trumpington Street, Cambridge CB2 1RP
40 West 20th Street, New York, NY 10011, USA
10 Stamford Road, Oakleigh, Melbourne 3166, Australia

© Cambridge University Press 1990

First published 1990

Printed in Great Britain by Scotprint, Musselburgh, Scotland

British Library cataloguing in publication data

Solomon, Nicky *1951 –*
Help your child with reading
1. Children, to 10 years. Reading skills. Teaching
I. Title
372.4

ISBN 0 521 33856 5

Designed by Claire Brodmann

Contents

Introduction

Chapter one	*Understanding reading*	7
Chapter two	*Your role as a parent*	14
Chapter three	*The pre-school child* (0 to 4 years)	17
	Reading to children	17
	Choosing suitable books	20
	Coping with difficulties	26
	Some answers to questions	27
Chapter four	*Beginning school* (5 to 6 years)	30
	Continuing with reading	30
	Choosing suitable books	32
	Working with the school	37
	Coping with difficulties	39
	Some answers to questions	40
Chapter five	*Gaining independence* (7 to 9 years)	44
	Listening to reading	44
	Working with the school	46
	Coping with difficulties	48
	Choosing suitable books	52
	Some answers to questions	58
Chapter six	*Developing reading* (10 years onwards)	62
	Reading non-fiction	62
	Increasing understanding	65
	Extending the range of books	68
	Coping with difficulties	74
	Some answers to questions	76
Chapter seven	*Summing up*	80
	Books for children	80
	Books for parents	91

Introduction

I share with most parents an interest in my children's education and like most parents I feel reading is particularly important.

I decided to write this book as a result of my own experience both as a teacher of reading and as a parent of two daughters, Emma and Kate. Over the past few years I have watched with delight my children's development as readers. They now display an enthusiasm towards reading that I believe will stay with them for the rest of their lives. I believe that our home has played an important part in this development.

Research has at last shown that parents play a major role in their children's education. It reveals that parental participation can be the significant single influence in a child's educational progress. This particularly so with reading, in terms of both ability and enjoyment.

This book is written for all parents, including those who are conf about the part they should play in their children's education, especi regard to reading. Often parents feel they *should* participate but dor confident enough to do so. The great mystique that surrounds readin makes people believe that you need special qualifications and training teach it. Some teachers still believe children need to be taught by professionals only and will suffer if untrained parents interfere in the process.

I don't agree with this. I believe that you as parents have both the right and the ability to help your children become good readers. But where do you go for advice? It may be difficult to approach the school. You may be concerned about troubling busy teachers, appearing pushy, sounding ignorant or interfering in something you know little about. So many of you questions go unanswered. This book will, I hope, provide at least some of the answers. Answers to questions like:

'Should I teach my child to read before she goes to school?'
'When do children start reading proper books?'
'Should I correct his mistakes?'
'How can I make reading enjoyable?'
'Are comics alright?'
'Should I force my child to read?
'How can I improve their comprehension?'

This book, with its explanation of the reading process and how it applies your child, will help you make sense of the conflicting views about readin that you may come across. Conflicts like:

- be involved, 'it doesn't hurt'   versus   don't be involved, 'leave it to
                                                      the professionals'

• teach children to read before they go to school, 'they'll do much better'	versus	wait or 'they'll be bored when they get there'
• wait until your child is 'ready'	versus	children are always ready
• teach them the alphabet first	versus	knowing the alphabet is not necessary for starting to read
• pictures are good	versus	pictures are no good, because they give them too many clues and that's not really reading
• encourage guessing	versus	guessing is no good, good readers don't guess
• good readers don't make mistakes	versus	good readers also make mistakes
• reading comics is not as good as reading books	versus	as long as children read, it doesn't matter what they read

Through this book I hope you will gain the knowledge that will enable you to play a more decisive role in your child's reading. It will demystify the reading process, offer practical guidelines to follow, and answer your questions.

Chapter one is about what is involved in reading. Chapter two is about your role as a parent in your child's development as a reader. Chapters three, four, five and six are divided into the different stages of development and as a matter of convenience have an age group range printed next to the chapter heading. However, these age divisions are very rough and should not be taken too seriously. Points raised in one particular chapter may be useful to you no matter if your child's age is above or below that given at the start of the chapter. Each stage of development depends so much on what has gone on before. For example, suitable reading materials for a seven year old can be found in chapter four as well as chapter five and the activities found in earlier chapters, such as reading to your child, should be considered as applying to all children.

I have included in each of chapters three to six a section on choosing suitable reading materials. This looks at the wide range of books available for different age groups. I have included many book titles. However, all the books mentioned, as well as those listed in chapter seven, are only a small sample of what you can buy.

Chapters three to six also contain sections which look at the problems that can arise, and also sections which give answers to a range of questions that parents often ask.

Chapters four and five contain sections on working together with the school. I have included these in order to highlight the important part a good home/school partnership plays in the development of our children as readers.

THE MICRO FILE

ALL RECIPES TESTED IN A 650-WATT MICROWAVE

Kidney Kebabs with Pilau Rice

Serves 4

Reader's report My 6 year old loved kidneys this way! Used easy-cook brown rice (3 min longer) for more fibre. Makes a nutritious meal.
Time prep 20 min/cook 24 min
Cost £1.90

1	large orange
8oz	(225g) easy-cook white rice
2oz	(50g) sultanas
½tsp	turmeric
1pt	(500ml) boiling water
1	green pepper
1lb	(450g) frozen lambs' kidneys, just thawed
2tbsp	oil

1. Cook on Full Power (100%) throughout. Peel away the orange rind with a zester or peel strips with a vegetable peeler, then cut into thin shreds. Cut 2 slices and reserve for garnish, from remaining

boiling water. Cover with cling film and peel back edge so steam can escape. Cook for 14 min stirring once, until water is absorbed and rice is tender.
3. Cut pepper in half. Core, deseed and cut into squares about ¾in (2cm).
4. Rinse and dry kidneys. Halve, strip away central core.
5. Thread folded kidneys and pepper alternately onto bamboo skewers. Prick kidneys well with a fine skewer and arrange kebabs in a single layer on a microproof plate. Brush with oil and sprinkle orange juice over. Cook for 8 min turning kebabs once during cooking.
6. Reheat rice for 2 min, spoon onto a plate and arrange the kebabs on top. Garnish with orange slices. Serve with a mixed leaf salad and chutney.

Nutrients per serving
Calories 420 Protein 23g
Total fat 11g (saturated fat 3g) Fibre 3g

Toad in the Hole

Serves 4

Reader's report Have never thought of microwaving this family favourite. Will make again as individual portions. Super midweek meal.
Time prep 10 min/cook 28 min
Cost £1.35

1lb	(450g) beef sausages
1	small onion, chopped
6oz	(150g) self-raising flour
2	eggs
½pt	(250ml) milk
½tsp	coarse-grain mustard

1. Cook on Full Power (100%) throughout. Preheat browning dish for 8 min or according to manufacturer's directions.
2. Put sausages on dish and cook for 6 min. Turn sausages over, add onion and cook for a further 3 min.
3. Transfer sausages and onion to a 2½pt (1.25 litre) shallow microproof dish.
4. Put flour into a bowl, add eggs and seasoning. Mix the milk with ¼pt (125ml) water

and mustard. Gradually add to the flour mixture, whisking until smooth.
5. Pour the batter around the sausages, cook, uncovered, for 8 min. until pudding is well risen. Transfer immediately to a preheated grill and cook for 2-3 min until golden brown. Serve immediately with baked beans or buttered cabbage.

Nutrients per serving
Calories 660 Protein 18g
Total fat 36g (saturated fat 15g) Carbohydrate 70g Fibre 3g

Micro tip: if you don't have a browning dish, grill sausages for 5-6 min until golden, turning occasionally.
Micro tip: for easy onion and mustard gravy, put 1 chopped onion, 1tbsp coarse-grain mustard, 2tsp cornflour and ½pt (250ml) beef stock in a jug. Cook on Full Power (100%) for 3-4 min, until thick, stirring thoroughly every minute.

Chapter One
Understanding reading

Many chapters in this book suggest practical guidelines for you to follow. While of course this might be just what you are looking for, these guidelines will make more sense if the mystique that surrounds the word 'reading' is removed. An understanding of how we ourselves read gives us a useful background for understanding how children learn to read. This understanding will enable you to help your child become and remain a good reader.

The word 'reading' means different things to different people. For some it might mean reading the newspaper or a novel while for others it might mean reading aloud. It can also mean the practical everyday skills needed for coping with tax forms and instructions on packets. This chapter explains what reading is by looking at why we read and what is involved in reading.

Why do we read?

The answer to this question may be clearer if you make a list of all the different things you have read in the last few days. Next to each one write down your reason for reading it. Here is my list.

Reading material	Reason
recipe for chocolate cake	wanted to try a new recipe
shopping list	checked to see if I had bought everything
telephone directory	looked up the dentist's phone number to make an appointment
novel	started reading a novel to relax
legal document	about to sign a lease for a new flat
note from school	wanted to find the date and the time of the parent/teacher interviews
TV guide	wanted to find out what time a certain programme started

This list, although it will be different from yours, reveals that we read all sorts of things for all sorts of reasons. Some of these are to find information, others are to check and confirm certain facts, while still others are for pleasure. Yet in spite of these different purposes, our reading does have something in common. In each reading task we are trying to understand a message that has been written down. If we can keep in mind that our goal in reading is *understanding meaning*, whatever we are reading or why, then we are one step closer to helping our children with their reading.

How do we read?
How do we
understand the
meaning?

What gives us the meaning is a *combination* of several factors.

What lies on the page
the letters, the words, the way the words are put together, pictures, layout,
logos, headlines, headings, letterheads, etc.

What we bring to reading
our knowledge of language (in this case English) and past experiences
with reading and with life.
    It isn't just one of these factors. Each plays an important part in the

reading process. However, some are more important than others. Try some of the following 'exercises' and you'll see what I mean.

The letters
Try reading this sentence:

We wen– to –he sho– to –uy –om– mi–k an– br–ad.

You can probably understand it although many of the letters are missing. The reason for this is that you are familiar with:

- the content of the sentence (buying bread and milk at the shops)
- the way the English words are put together to make up a sentence
- the combination of letters that make up words

Certainly you have to have some of the letters, but you didn't need them all. You were able to predict what the sentence said by combining what was there on the page with your knowledge of language and the world.

The words
Now try reading this sentence:

Christmas day falls _____ the 25th _____.

Although some of the words are missing you can probably read the sentence. Again, this is so because you have combined your knowledge of the content (this time of Christmas), your knowledge of the English language (eg. 25th is usually followed by a month) and with the letters that were supplied, to arrive at the meaning.

The way the words are put together

Try to 'read' the following passage and then answer the questions.

Zing quackles and randles estrates were zickled. While zickling the quackles frumbled, zooped and finally predacked. All quackles generally predack, but if immigted prior to zickling, they sometimes will not predack and may only frumble and zoop.

What were zickled?
What happened to them during zickling?
How can you try to prevent predacking?

You are probably able to answer the questions because the words have been put together in the same way as they are in normal English. You may even be able to read the passage aloud because many of the letters are combined just as they are in ordinary English words, for example 'ickled' and 'umble'. However, it is unlikely that you could understand it. This is because you don't know the words themselves, so there is no *meaning*.

Clues

Isolated words, or even sentences and paragraphs, can be extremely difficult to understand if you don't know what the background is. But once you do know the background, or the context, you can get some important clues as to the meaning.

For example try reading this sentence:

> Where a reading of a meter cannot be made for the purpose of rendering an account because of the absence of access to the meter, the account may bear an estimated reading instead of the actual reading.

Now read it in context:

The Australian Gas Light Company
AGL Centre
Cnr Pacific Highway & Walker Street
North Sydney NSW 2060
Telephone 922 8000

Dear Customer,
The quarterly routine reading of your gas meter and/or hot water meter is scheduled to take place on **THURSDAY, 4 SEP** . . . .

We would appreciate you arranging for someone to admit a Company Representative on that date, or please complete the reverse side of this card and LEAVE IT ON OR AT YOUR FRONT DOOR BEFORE 7.30 a.m.
Please note: Where a reading of a meter cannot be made for the purpose of rendering an account because of the absence of access to the meter, the account may bear an estimated reading instead of the actual reading.
(Regulations under The Gas and Electricity Act.)

5145/3/84

When the sentence was isolated you didn't know what it was about so it was hard to tell the meaning. However, the second time round clues from the context allowed you to draw on your experience and knowledge. Experience with the gas company, with paying bills in general, and with receiving a card like this one, can help you to predict what it is about and makes the message easier to understand. However, if you've never seen a card like this in your life before the context won't help you, because you won't have the background knowledge to predict what the print says.

Reading strategies   Another important thing to remember about reading is that we don't read everything the same way. Sometimes, to get the message, we read every word. Sometimes we only read certain parts, while at other times we just glance through the whole. It depends on why we're reading it and whether we've read that kind of thing before or not. At the beginning of this chapter you made a list of some of the things you have read during the last few days and noted the reasons for reading them. If you went back to that list and beside each entry made a further note of how you went about reading it your list might now look like this:

Reading material	Reason	Reading strategy
recipe for chocolate cake	wanted to try a new recipe	needed to read it a few times
shopping list	checked to see if I had bought everything	looked through it quickly
telephone directory	looked up the dentist's phone number to make an appointment	used my knowledge of the alphabet and how the telephone directory works to find it
novel	for relaxation	read it quickly
legal document	about to sign a lease	looked quickly through it and then read certain parts slowly and carefully
note from school	wanted to find the date and the time of the parent/teacher interviews	looked for specific information
TV guide	checked time of programme	looked for specific information

7

5.50: The Tomorrow People — (Rpt).
6.20: Leave It To Beaver — (Rpt, b/w).
6.45: Cartoon Connection — (Rpts).
9.00: Romper Room — For tots.
10.00: Falcon Crest — (PGR, Rpt).
11.00: Eleven AM — Topical show.
12.00: Movie — The Seven Year Itch (PGR, 55, Rpt). Billy Wilder directed this classic comedy about a married man, left alone when his family take summer holiday, who discovers

ABC

8.00: Mr Squiggle And Friends — (Rpt).
8.30: Sesame Street. **9.30:** Play School — (*S). **10.00:** Daytime Programs.
1.00: News. **1.05:** Daytime Programs.
3.00: Sesame Street. **3.55:** Magic Roundabout. **4.00:** Play School — (*S).
4.30: Captain Cookaburra's Road To Discovery — (Rpt). **4.55:** Captain Pugwash. **5.00:** Inspector Gadget (Rpt).
5.25: Roger Ram

9

6.00: News And Weather.
6.30: Today. (6.40: Business Today).
9.00: Here's Humphrey — (Rpt).
10.00: The Young Doctors — (Rpt).
10.30: General Hospital — (PGR).
11.30: Morning News. **12.00:** Midday Show With Ray Martin — (PGR).
1.30: Daytime Serials (PGR).

BBC 1

6.0 am Ceefax AM. **6.30** The Flintstones. **6.55** Weather. **7.0** Breakfast Time. **8.55** Regional News. **9.0** News; Open Air. **9.20** Kilroy! **10.0** News; Dr Kildare. **10.25** Children's BBC: Playbus (R). **10.50** Stoppit and Tidyup (R). **10.55** Five to Eleven. **11.0** News: Open Air. **12.0** News; World Snooker. **12.55** Regional News. **1.0** News; Weather. **1.30** Neighbours. **1.50** World Snooker.

2.15 Knots Landing: Four. No Trump.
3.0 Now Get Out of That. Continuing the outdoor survival challenge between Oxford and Cambridge teams (R).
3.50 Children's BBC: Corners (R). **4.5** Mysterious Cities of

BBC 2

6.55-7.20 am Open University: Carmel — A World Within. **9.0** Ceefax pages. **9.45** Daytime on Two. Economics — A Question of Choice. **10.5** You and Me; **10.20** Science Workshop: **10.40** Textile Studies; **11.0** Words and Pictures; **11.15** Walrus; **11.35** The Geography Programme. **11.55** A-Level German, **12.15** Big Top Science; **12.35** Lifeschool; **1.0** Business Matters. **1.25** Green Claws (R) **1.40** Zig Zag (R). **2.0** News; Weather; Storyteller (R).

2.15 World Snooker. David Icke with further quarter-final coverage from The Crucible, including **3.50** News, Weather; **3.50** News. Weather; Regional News.

ITV London

5.0 am ITN Morning News. **6.0** TV-am. **9.25** Keynotes. **9.55** Local news; weather. **10.0** The Time The Place. **10.40** This Morning including **10.55** News headlines. **11.55** Local news headlines. **12.10** Allsorts (R). **12.30** A Country Practice. **1.0** News; weather. **1.20** Local news; weather.

1.30 Something to Treasure. The collectors' magazine goes backstage at Christie's.
2.0 Richmond Hill.
3.0 Tell the Truth. **3.25** Local news; weather.
3.30 Sons and Daughters.
4.0 Children's ITV: The Moomins. **4.5** The Raggy Dolls.

Channel 4

6.0 am The Channel 4 Daily. **9.25** Schools. **9.30** The French Programme. **9.52** Environments. **10.9** All Year Round. **10.26** Facts for Life. **10.48** Believe It or Not! **11.5** Middle English; **11.22** Picture Box; **11.41** Craft, Design and Technology. **12.0** The Parliament Programme. **12.30** Business Daily. **1.0** Open College: The Customer Connection — Who Cares Wins ★ (R). **1.30** Working Words. ★ (R). **2.0** Sesame Street.

2.30 Channel 4 Racing from Epsom, introduced by Brough Scott.
4.30 Fifteen-to-One.
5.0 Go for It. Last of the lively series, following one group of youngsters on a rock climbing expedition in

Your list, like the one above, probably reveals a range of different reading strategies. The particular strategy used for each of the different reading materials depends on what you were reading, your familiarity with its content and language, and the purpose you had for reading it. For example, checking to see if you have bought everything on your shopping list certainly needs a different approach from reading a lease for a house or flat. With a lease you may not know what kind of information it contains and you'll probably be unfamiliar with the type of language used. This, combined with being rather concerned about signing something which involves a large amount of money, means you need to focus on the print. So you read it slowly and perhaps re-read certain parts in order to make sure that you have got it right. However, with the shopping list it is likely that you wrote it yourself. Therefore you have a fair idea what's in it, and a quick glance would probably be sufficient.

Characteristics of good readers

Another way of understanding what is involved in reading is to look at what 'good' readers do when they are reading. As this chapter has shown, even good readers like us find some things difficult to read, and certainly when faced with unfamiliar material our reading slows down. There are, however, certain characteristics that 'good' readers have in common:

- concern with meaning rather than making sounds
- reading quickly and not focussing on every letter or word
- leaving out unknown words when fluency is more important than accuracy
- using different reading strategies depending on the content and purpose for reading it
- paying attention only to the relevant information
- guessing and predicting ahead
- looking quickly through something unfamiliar before reading it in detail
- picking up key words to get an idea of what it is about
- making mistakes in reading and correcting these only when the meaning is lost

Just to highlight some of these points, you might like to try reading aloud the following passage (without first reading it silently to yourself):

The boys' arrows were nearly gone so they sat down on the grass and stopped hunting. Over at the edge of the wood they saw Henry making a bow to a small girl who was coming down the road. She had tears in her dress and tears in her eyes. She gave Henry a note which he brought over to the group of young hunters. Read to the boys it caused great excitement. After a minute but rapid examination of their weapons they ran down to the valley. Does were standing at the edge of the lake, making an excellent target.

Did you hesitate at all? Did you make any mistakes?
Did you add, substitute or leave out any words? If so, was the meaning lost or kept?
Did you correct any mistakes?
Did you re-read certain parts?

Even as a good reader you probably made several mistakes. You may have misread the words 'bow', 'tear', 'read', 'minute', 'does'. For example, with the word 'bow' you probably used 'arrows' as a clue, yet it didn't make sense, so to get the meaning you needed to re-read certain parts or read on for more clues.

This passage was deliberately written so as to encourage those mistakes and, of course, most of what you read does not have such traps. Also, when we read silently to ourselves, we are not always so aware of what we are doubtful about or of the mistakes we make. All the same, it does show that reading isn't an accurate process. We leave words out, we add others and we correct ourselves. We do all these things to try to get meaning from something that has been written down.

In the following chapters I suggest what you can do to help your child to become an active reader. Like us, children need to understand what they are reading. And, like us, their knowledge and experience interact with what is written on the page.

Chapter Two

Your role as a parent

Reading, once seen as a skill to be taught at school, is actually something that starts at home. It is rooted in a child's spoken language and life experiences, from its earliest days. Before looking at how children learn to read, it is interesting to note the informal way children learn to speak.

Children learn to speak by speaking and being spoken to, and not by a formal teaching programme. From birth, children are surrounded by meaningful language and they soon learn that spoken words have meaning. We eagerly await our children's first words, accepting and encouraging their early attempts at speech. We are usually not worried about it being 'baby talk' and not 'real' language. On the contrary, we respond to their noises and sounds in an encouraging way, not only with praise (and occasional applause) but also by replying to what they say, no matter how it is said.

How does this relate to learning to read?

Previously many people believed that written language was separate and unrelated to spoken language. It was felt that learning to read, unlike learning to speak, involved the mastery of a set of specific skills. It began with the letters of the alphabet, moved on to the sounds represented by the letters, then to simple words, then to complex words and so on. However, nowadays reading, writing, listening and speaking are seen as parallel language skills. It is now recognised that the learning conditions which help your child to learn to read are similar to those that helped him or her learn to speak.

Home rather than school is the place where learning to read begins. Your child does not wait until a formal teaching programme starts before learning to read. From birth, children are surrounded by meaningful print. Most children are exposed to many different kinds of print, such as signs, advertisements, newspapers and books. In fact, they become aware of print as soon as it is relevant to them. They very quickly realise that print has a purpose and that this purpose and its message are related to its context. For example the Macdonalds sign tells them that a Macdonalds restaurant is close by and a Stop sign tells them that you have to stop the car at the junction. Very young children can read print when it is relevant to them and when the purpose and message are clear.

Just as you didn't need special tools or kits when your child was learning to speak, you likewise don't need them for helping with reading. You don't need books offering guidelines to follow on which sounds or words your child should say first. Children don't learn meaningless 'bits' of language – speaking and meaning go together. The same applies with learning to read. Many of the 'teach your child to read' kits that are available tend to focus on isolated words and phrases and lay down hard and fast rules about what to do. I'm sure many of you have heard the success stories told by parents who have 'taught' their child to read using these prepackaged kits. I believe that these children learnt to read not because of the kits but because of everything else that the parents were doing at the same time – everyday activities like reading books to them, telling them stories and providing a stimulating home environment where reading is encouraged and enjoyed.

Before children go to school they often have a fairly good idea about reading and how to read, even though no-one has sat down and 'taught' them. This is true not just for exceptional children but also for those who are surrounded by the printed word in and around the home, and who see reading as a useful part of the world in which they live. It's useful to remember just how much children are able to understand about reading from a very early age. Here are some reminders.

- Children usually know very well that something written means something. For example, they point to and read the bus stop sign, the train station name or the title of their favourite book.
- Children soon come to understand that we don't read everything the same way. They see us absorbed in an interesting newspaper article, or just flicking through the mail, looking up a number in the telephone directory, or quickly taking in a telephone message someone has left for us.
- Children know very quickly that it isn't just the letters that matter and look for clues in the context. For example, they can read a badly weathered bus stop sign, a telephone box sign without the first four letters or the toilet sign without the middle 'I'.
- Children can also see that we often look at the pictures before reading something or while we are reading it, such as when we read magazines or when we read a story in a picture book.
- They know that sometimes we make mistakes when we read aloud, that we leave words out, add some and even change some. How often do we hear our children say, 'But you left out this line!' or 'It doesn't say that!' when we are reading their favourite stories?
- Children hear us guessing or predicting what a story or article is about, before we read it and while we're reading it. For example, before we even open a letter, we might say, 'Oh no! Not another bill!' or 'I bet this is from Sue – I'm sure she's got some news this time.'
- Children know that we read things for particular reasons. For example, we might read a label on some winter pyjamas to find out if they are flammable or we might read a newspaper article to find out about the weather forecast.

When parents encourage this awareness and understanding as well as using the natural learning conditions that exist when children learn to speak, children will learn to read and become good readers. As a parent, you have the qualities and skills which are extremely valuable to your child's learning. Your home provides numerous opportunities for your children to see the function and value of print. It is in the home that children begin to see the amount of pleasure and information reading can give. With security, opportunities, encouragement and support, you can help your children approach reading as an enjoyable and meaningful activity and something they will want to do. There are four general points following on how you can best support and encourage your child's development as a reader. These points appear in more detail in the later chapters.

Regular reading You can help most by **reading to your children** regularly and by continuing to do so even after they have learnt to read. You'll be able to choose books and stories that will appeal to them – and you will have a captive audience. You can increase their reading resources by taking them with you to the library and bookshops and also by taking advantage of the magazines, newspapers, and TV and radio programmes lying around at home. As your children get older you can *listen to them read*. Encourage them, praise them, accept their mistakes and don't worry that they'll never get it right.

Talk and listen By encouraging them to put their thoughts and feelings into words you can help them develop their language and build up their vocabulary. This in turn develops their reading skills and confidence. It is difficult in the rush of daily life to set time aside to talk to your child but there are lots of small things you can do which don't take much time or effort at all.

- Try to give your children a few minutes when they get back from playgroup or school to tell you what's been going on.
- Try to link up books you read to your children with their own lives. For example, if the book is about a day at the zoo you could talk about your last family visit to the zoo.
- When the family is watching television, talk about what you are watching and what might happen next.

Ration TV This does not mean banning TV altogether, but it is important to encourage your children to be more discriminating in their choice of programmes and more critical of what they watch. Try and get them to plan in advance the programmes they want to see. It might be good for you to do a bit more of that yourself as an example!

Read yourself It helps if children see you reading. If you like reading then it is likely that your child will too.

Chapter Three
The pre-school child (0 to 4 years)

In this chapter I want to give help in how to encourage your pre-school child's learning by providing a home reading environment. At this age, the two best ways of doing this are reading to your child and choosing suitable materials.

Reading to children

Reading to your children is one of the easiest and most useful ways of helping them learn to read and to love reading. You are probably already doing this, yet you may not realise just how valuable it is. It almost seems too simple, but it's true. By reading frequently and regularly to your children from a very young age, you are helping them learn many things about books and stories, about reading and about life. The earlier you start, the earlier they will discover the pleasures of reading.

By watching you read, children learn to behave like readers. They learn how to handle books, where a book starts and ends, and how the pages turn with the story line. They will probably want to imitate your behaviour with books and you should give them the chance to do so. Certainly a young baby who has just learnt to grab and hold (if not tear and eat!) everything in sight, will want to do the same with this wonderful new object – a book! However just because your child, if given the chance, may rip the odd book apart, it doesn't mean he or she is not interested in books or is too young. Remember, your child's favourite teddy bear or cuddly is rarely totally destroyed by over-anxious little fingers. With the right books you can soon capture your child's interest, especially if you show your enthusiasm. You can also try to give your baby something to chew on, while he or she listens to you reading. It can be so pleasurable to see how their eyes wait in anticipation for the page to turn.

By listening to you read, children learn the pattern of stories and the type of language used to carry these stories along. Young children soon learn that a story has a beginning, a middle and an end. My children will rarely let me stop reading a story half way through; they insist that I finish it. They have to hear the ending, even if they have heard it many times before. Children also soon learn the type of language that is used in stories, especially those phrases that signify the beginnings and endings. Even very young children will join in with phrases like 'once upon a time . . .' and 'they lived happily ever after'. They also learn what to expect from story characters. Handsome princes and helpful fairies with magic wands are eagerly awaited and inevitably turn up. These characters stay with children for a long time and play an important part in their fantasies and imaginative play and, as they get older, in the stories they write.

They become familiar with the words we use when talking about books. Knowledge of words, such as 'top of the page', 'bottom left hand corner', 'author' and 'illustrator' can help them find books they want and talk about parts of the story or pictures that interest them. It also prepares them for the language that they will hear at school.

When you read to children they are learning to understand what gives the stories meaning. First, they can see that you don't read letter by letter and that you may even leave some words out. This is especially obvious to them if they are familiar with the story, and they will often say, 'but you left out that bit about the fairy!' when you try to hurriedly read their favourite story. They also learn how the illustrations, together with the words, provide the meaning. *Rosie's Walk* by Pat Hutchins is a good example of a book in which the illustrations provide a vital part of the story. There is no mention of the fox in the words, yet his presence plays an important role in the story.

Children learn that reading is very pleasurable. The pleasure and companionship which books and stories offer are a wonderful motivation for them to read themselves. This pleasure can come from the content of the story, the illustrations, and the language in which the stories are written. Books can provide your children with many experiences. They learn about other people and about themselves. Some stories can prepare them for experiences in their own lives such as a bus or train trip, or a visit to the dentist. Others provide experiences they may never encounter, like life on a farm or the discovery of long lost treasure. Some stories can help children understand and feel better about themselves by acknowledging their own thoughts, fears and emotions. It is very comforting for children to see that they are not alone in their fears of the dark or of spiders. My elder daughter reread *There's a Sea in My Bedroom* by Margaret Wild (Nelson), many times. The first time she read it she felt so much better having shared her fear about the sea. She returned to it often, possibly to relive the comfort that she felt.

Books and stories not only broaden the children's world but can also enrich their language. The language of books can help children express their own feelings and thoughts, and provide different words to say different things. I heard with delight my own daughter mumbling, 'Scrumptious!' as she chomped her way through dinner following the fifth reading in a row (her own choice) of *The Lighthouse Keeper's Lunch* by David and Ronda Armitage.

Reading to children can also bring you closer to them. It provides an opportunity for a 'quiet' time where both you and your child can share the events of the book or relive any real life experience that may have been triggered by the story.

Reading books to your children can do all these things – but they don't happen overnight. It does require time and effort. Although there may be times when your child is not interested or when you just haven't got the energy, there will be times which make it all worthwhile, such as the first time your child reads quietly to him- or herself or starts to read to you. There is no doubt that children who grow up having books read to them when they are young, learn to appreciate books and reading much more than those who don't. The following points may help you and your child enjoy the time you spend together with books.

- With very young children there is always the danger they will tear the pages either through ignorance of how to handle a book or an over-enthusiasm to get on with it. However, the more chances they have to handle books the quicker they will learn how to do it. Meanwhile, keep the more expensive ones out of reach, and the more durable board books where children can pick them up.
- Reading books should be an enjoyable experience. Try to make the time you spend reading to your child relaxing and tension-free. Easier said than done, I know. The time needs to be suitable for both you and your child and not when a favourite TV show is on, when your child's friends are waiting outside or when you are cooking dinner and thinking about the hundreds of other things you have to do in the next hour. Reading should be a pleasure, not a duty.
- Talking to children about the story can help them recall their own experiences, which in turn help them understand the story. Talking and reading often go on throughout the story time. It is quite natural that children will interrupt and add extra details or ask the inevitable, 'why?' and 'where?' questions. You too may want to stop during parts of a story to discuss interesting things. Perhaps it is something that happened in another story or something that happened to you. *Harry the Dirty Dog* by Gene Zion was a long-time favourite in our home because it reminded us of Sooty, our real-life dirty dog, and gave us an opportunity to talk about her. You may also want to encourage your children to guess what a story is about, both before you start and while you are reading it, to compare these ideas with what actually happens. This will help their prediction skills by encouraging them to think about the story in advance. This doesn't mean you should do this with every book, but occasionally it is a good idea.
- Reading with a child works better if you both get some interest and fun out of it. Fortunately there are many excellent picture books available today which are interesting for both adult and child. But, of course, children sometimes fasten on to stories that are boring to adults, and even good books may lose their adult appeal on the sixth reading. Nevertheless bear with it and keep in mind that another, hopefully better, favourite book is just around the corner.
- Give your child a chance to choose a book to read. Children need to have some control over what they want to read and this provides an important impetus to continue reading.
- Although it may be irritating at times, try not to discourage your child from joining in. Children may like to 'read' the last word of every page or sentence and it is a good idea to encourage this. Some books, because of

their predictable rhyme and repetition, actually invite this joining in and children feel good about it.

- Don't assume that because your children are active and can't sit still for a minute that books couldn't possibly hold their attention. Reading a book to an active child may be just what is needed. It can also be an easy time-filler. Many difficult moments can be avoided in such places as a doctor's waiting room, by reading a favourite story to a child who is otherwise likely to create havoc.

Choosing suitable books

Today there is an enormous range of books available for pre-school children. We can now find books not only in bookshops and libraries but in newsagents and supermarkets as well. This is certainly a good thing, but having so much to choose from can often be daunting. This section and the booklist in chapter seven will, I hope, help you and your children in your choice. Also, don't be afraid to ask your local librarian and bookshop assistant for advice. Their experiences with a wide range of ages and needs can be extremely useful.

What are suitable books for pre-school children?

Picture books come first to mind when thinking about suitable books for pre-school children. By picture books I mean not books just with pictures of objects, but books in which the pictures and the words together tell a story, however simple. *Pictures* are what you look at first in a picture book, so it is important that they should be immediately attractive to a child. They can provide a wonderful stimulus for discussion as well as helping to keep the interest in the story going. It is also important that the pictures are closely related to the words, so that together they carry the story. Good pictures can let children 'read' a book on their own, which helps them to see themselves as readers from a very young age. Children learn to use pictures to predict the story and to expand the meaning of the words. Both my children, as soon as they could say a few words, would confidently sit up in their cots turning the pages of their favourite book. At first they would just occasionally name the objects on the page and then as they got older they would retell the story using the pictures as their cues. Sometimes the story would be the same as the one I had just read, while at other times they would tell it in a different way.

The language in picture books needs to be largely familiar to the child. However, this doesn't mean that the book needs to be written in basic English or restricted to the language your child uses when speaking. In fact, for several reasons this would not be a good thing. For a start, written language is generally different in some degree to the language we speak. Secondly, we should not assume that children don't understand words because they don't say them. This leads on to the third reason as the language in books can enrich children's own language, especially if they are able to relate to the events or characters of the story. Another important point about the language used is that, just as good pictures draw your child into the story, so can the language. Rhymes, repetitions, rhythm and build-up lines all provide an irresistible invitation to your child to join in. Who can resist joining in with 'Good grief!' said the goose. 'Well, well!' said the pig. 'Who cares?' said the sheep. 'So what?' said the horse. 'What next?' said the cow. etc. in Mem Fox's delightful *Hattie and the Fox?* Lines like these strike a chord in children and draw them back to the story time and time again.

Below you will find a guide to the types of picture books that are suitable for different age groups, from very young babies to five year olds. It is a rough guide only and is based on books and types of books that have been very successful with my own children and their friends. Of course, what you and your child choose to read will depend on your child's age, interests and experiences both with life and with books, all of which are constantly changing.

Whatever books you and your child choose, keep in mind the following:

- Your aim is not to use books to teach your child to read but rather to create a love for books so that reading becomes an enjoyable, informative part of life.
- The interaction between you, your child and the book is even more important than the choice of books. How you read to your child and the talk that arises before, during and after can contribute so much more.
- It is important to offer a range of different types of books, such as poems, fairy tales and other stories. Each of these has a particular style. Not only do children enjoy the variety but it is useful for them to get to know the different conventions that belong to each one.
- As children get older, they naturally like to choose their own books. While it is important that they are allowed to do so, it is equally important that we offer them a hand. Show children that the front and back covers, the title and the pictures, all provide information that can help them make a choice.

Very young children – under two's Generally, very young children enjoy theme books. These books don't have a story but contain pictures of objects, people, animals or things that are connected in some way. They also love alphabet, colour and number books which have large colourful pictures of familiar objects. Some of the many titles include:
Baby's Catalogue:Peepo by Janet and Allan Ahlberg (Picture/Puffin)
ABC; *Colours*; *Numbers*; *Home*; *Shapes*; *Sizes*; *Time*; *Weather* by Jan Pienkowski (Heinemann/Puffin)
Little Numbers; *Little Wheels* by Rodney Peppé (Methuen)

They love books which are about the daily events of their lives, such as bathtime, mealtimes and getting dressed time. For example:
How Do I Put It On?; *I Can Build a House*; *I Can Do It!* by Shigeo Watanabe (Bodley Head/Puffin)
Bathwater's Hot; *Noisy*; *When We Went to the Park* by Shirley Hughes (Walker Books)

They love books which encourage noise making – especially those which encourage them to make the noise of a particular animal, such as in:
Goodnight Owl by Pat Hutchins (Puffin/Penguin)
Old MacDonald Had a Farm illustrated by Tracey Campbell Pearson (Bodley Head)

They love books where they can make things happen and/or guess where things are, such as in:
Are You There, Bear?; *Is Anyone Home?* by Ron Maris (Julia MacRae)
Where's Spot? by Eric Hill (Puffin/Penguin)
Anybody Home?; *Where's My Baby?* by H.A. Rey (Bodley Head)

Books which contain nursery rhymes and songs are always popular. The repetition and the rhyme invite your child to join in. They also have the advantage of being very easy to learn by heart. This can save many dull moments and can serve as a wonderful diversion on long car drives or the seemingly endless wait for a bottle of milk to warm up. There are numerous publications available but here are just a few good examples:
Lavender's Blue compiled by Kathleen Lines and Harold Jones (Oxford)
This Little Puffin compiled by Elizabeth Matterson (Puffin/Penguin)
Rhymes Around the Day by Jan Ormerod (Puffin/Penguin)

Two year olds The types of books and the individual books mentioned above are still suitable for two year olds. However, because your two year old is becoming more independent and because his or her world is expanding and language is developing, a wider range of books is now suitable. Your child will now be able to follow stories, be involved with the characters in a story and be interested in what happens in other people's lives. The story line should still be quite simple and have a predictable outcome. Nothing gives a two year old greater pleasure than hearing a story unfold exactly as he or she guessed.

Two year olds love stories that realistically portray the familiar experiences and excitement in their lives. Some examples are:
Alfie's Feet; *An Evening at Alfie's*; *Lucy and Tom at the Seaside* by Shirley Hughes (Bodley Head)
Titch by Pat Hutchins (Puffin)
Thomas and Emma books by Guilla Wolde (Hodder & Stoughton)

Two year olds love books where the language invites their involvement and participation, such as by the use of rhythm and rhymes in poems and nursery rhymes, and the repetitive and cumulative words and lines in some stories. Some examples are:
Each Peach, Pear, Plum by Janet and Allan Ahlberg (Kestrel/Puffin)
Bertie the Bear; *Who Sank the Boat?* by Pamela Allen (Nelson)
The Very Hungry Caterpillar by Eric Carle (Puffin/Penguin)

Three year olds Three year olds will enjoy the types of books already mentioned. However, because they are now a year older the stories can be more sophisticated.

Below are some examples of some books that fit into the above categories but are more complex.

Familiar experiences
Don't Forget the Bacon; *You'll Soon Grow Into Them Titch*; *Happy Birthday Sam* by Pat Hutchins (Puffin/Penguin)
Sunshine; *Moonlight* by Jan Ormerod (Puffin/Penguin)

Repetition
The Wind Blew by Pat Hutchins (Puffin/Penguin)
Would You Rather? (Lion); *Mr Gumpy's Motor Car*; *Mr Gumpy's Outing* (Puffin) by John Burningham

Fun and adventure
Harry the Dirty Dog; *Harry by the Sea* by Gene Zion (Bodley Head)
The Tiger Who Came to Tea by Judith Kerr (Picture Lions)
Possum Magic by Mem Fox (Omnibus)

Your three year old is also likely to demand a larger say in what books you choose to read to him or her. While accommodating children's wishes and tastes you can now offer them a wider selection. You can introduce folk and fairy tales, but please be careful as some are unsuitable. Read each one before you read it to your child to make sure that it is suitable. Some fairy tales are quite violent and others are very disturbing. In my over-enthusiasm to share my own childhood stories with my eldest daughter I fear I unwittingly destroyed fairy tales for her forever. As a three year old, her night-time fears of monsters and beasts were not exactly calmed by 'Beauty and the Beast'. Now even at the age of ten, she is still a little hesitant about reading anything that resembles a fairy tale. Nevertheless if you are selective they can be suitable. Three year olds enjoy folk tales like 'The Gingerbread Man', 'The Three Billy Goats Gruff', 'Henny Penny' and 'Goldilocks and the Three Bears'. Some suitable fairy tales are 'The Elves and the Shoemaker', 'The Emperor's New Clothes' and 'The Ugly Duckling'.

There are many suitable picture book stories that explore children's fears and feelings of rivalry, jealousy and being left out. Children like to know that other children suffer similarly and they can learn from these books that many of their fears can be overcome.
Timothy Goes to School; *Noisy Nora* by Rosemary Wells (Puffin/Penguin)
Knock, Knock, Who's There? by Sally Grindley (Hamish Hamilton)
Angela's New Sister by Janet Matarasso (Cambridge)
Arannea by Jenny Wagner (Puffin)

Books that prepare them for a coming event can also be very useful. There are many books about a new baby, starting pre-school, a visit to the doctor or dentist, a stay in hospital, etc. Even after the event, children will return to these books which, like the ones above, provide reassurance that things get better. Althea's books, *Visiting the Dentist*, *Going to the Doctor*, and *Going into Hospital* (Dinosaur Books) are examples of this type.

Four year olds These older pre-school children have many favourites which they return to again and again. But now is the time for introducing new stories that can be longer and more complex. They can expand your children's world while at the same time make them laugh and reassure them that their lives and feelings are experienced by others. Many of the characters in realistic stories are animals rather than people. These can be both fun in themselves and also, by the fact that they are **not** people, enable your child to 'feel' with them more easily. It is also a good idea to read books that develop their imagination. Such books can prepare children for the fantasy stories and fairy tales that they will read later on.

More examples
Again I have divided the titles of books into similar categories as in the three year old group. However, many of them have characteristics of each and most are accompanied by a good laugh.

Fun and adventure
The Enormous Crocodile by Roald Dahl (Puffin)
A Lighthouse Keeper's Lunch (Puffin/Penguin); *The Lighthouse Keeper's Catastrophe* (Andre Deutsch) by Ronda and David Armitage

Feelings
Willy the Wimp; *Willy the Champ* by Anthony Browne (J. MacRae Books)
The Very Worst Monster by Pat Hutchins (Bodley Head)
John Brown, Rose and the Midnight Cat by Jenny Wagner (Puffin)

Everyday experiences
Ernest and Celestine; *Merry Christmas, Ernest and Celestine*; *Bravo, Ernest and Celestine* by Gabrielle Vincent (Picture Lions/Armada)

Repetition
Chicken Licken by Jan Ormerod (Walker Books)
The Doorbell Rang by Pat Hutchins (Bodley Head)

Imagination
Where the Wild Things Are by Maurice Sendak (Puffin/Penguin)
A Dark, Dark Tale by Ruth Brown (Hippo)
Felix and Alexander by Terry Denton (Oxford)

Poetry
I feel poetry is an extremely valuable addition to all pre-school children's reading and listening experiences. Like nursery rhymes, poems give rise to a love and feel for language. The rhymes and rhythm are easily

remembered and invite children to join in. Many poems reflect children's moods and feelings and help them express these. Other poems are just plain fun. Some invaluable poetry books for pre-schoolers are:

A Very First Poetry Book compiled by John Louis Foster (Oxford)
Don't Put Mustard in the Custard by Michael Rosen and Quentin Blake (Andre Deutsch)

Materials other than published books

Real life reading materials

There is an enormous amount of print in and around the home which children are reading all the time, just because it is part of the family's everyday life. Every family is different. In some the regular reading may be the newspaper and the football results, in others a computer user's handbook and a weekly gardening magazine, in yet others books from the library or the latest paperback. It doesn't really matter. If your child sees you reading in and around the home he or she will follow in your footsteps.

As your child gets older signs on the streets and in the shops start to mean more. Before long your child will point to a sign and shout out 'exit', 'wet paint' and the name of your street or suburb. Encourage your child in attempts to make sense of the printed words all around. If your child shows an interest, let him or her help you choose a birthday card for Gran, find the tomato sauce in the supermarket, find his or her birthday in a calendar and tell you who the letter that has just arrived is for.

Making children's books

Homemade children's books can be a welcome addition to your child's home library. Pre-school children love reading stories prompted by photos of family outings, holidays, pets etc., and about adventures and feelings that they have experienced. Reading a story about themselves, perhaps written down by you in their own words, can give them great pleasure.

There are several ways in which children can write their own stories. How you choose to do it and when you do it, depends on your child's motivation, interests and needs. Some children aren't interested and others enjoy it. Some children initiate it themselves, others may need some encouragement. Some children start to 'write' stories from the moment they can hold a pencil while others always want you to do their writing. Whichever way it is, remember that the point is not to teach your child how to write, but to help him or her enjoy reading and learn how to make sense of stories. Here are a couple of suggestions for how you might set about it.

You act as scribe

Your child, prompted by a photo, picture or drawing, tells you a story. You write down the story as your child tells it to you. Stick to the language that the child uses, as it is not a time for correcting grammar. At the same time it doesn't mean that you should write all the 'ums' and 'ahs'. It is all right to make changes, especially if the meaning is unclear, but be careful to keep the child's language and story line. Your child might want to illustrate the story, before or after it is written. That can make it much more his or her **own** story. Read the story back to your child and check if that is what he or she intended.

Your child does the writing

This time the child prompted by a photo, picture or drawing, writes their story. Of course if your child is very young this writing may be indecipherable and may be only squiggles. However, it isn't a handwriting or spelling lesson and if your child is able to 'read' it back to you, then accept it. Some children may be quite happy with their writing attempts, while others may want you to write the 'correct' form under theirs. Again, illustration makes it more personal to the child.

It is a good idea to staple together your child's stories (dated perhaps?) together with the pictures. The stories can become a book and will probably be a cherished one. It is important to keep these points in mind.

- Your child needs to continue to read other books. Published stories provide good models for children and they need to see the patterns and shapes of different stories. It helps them with their own story telling.
- Don't pressure your child to produce long stories. Leave it up to him or her. Sometimes your child might have a lot to say, while at other times may simply want to write a few words.
- Your child doesn't have to 'read' every word that has been written down. It is not a test to see if he or she can get every word right.
- Keep the stories whole. Don't cut the stories up into sentences or separate phrases and ask your child to put it back together. Don't test if the words can be read out of context.

Coping with difficulties

All the suggestions so far may sound easy but are perhaps not always so easy to put into practice. You probably feel that it is fine for those whose children are always willing to cooperate or who have all the time in the world. But of course this is not always so. What can you do if your child is just not interested in books and if you are too exhausted even to think about reading to your child?

Not interested

Most of us at some time experience the difficulties of dealing with a child who is just not interested or who is uncooperative. Perhaps your child refuses to sit still, perhaps he or she talks over you or perhaps just simply doesn't pay attention. Whatever it is, it can be extremely frustrating. Sometimes no matter how hard we try, our children aren't interested and don't cooperate. Not even a wonderful selection of books or an enthusiastic story telling seems to work. But all is not lost. It doesn't mean your child will never read and above all it doesn't mean that you are an unsuccessful parent. Remember every child is an individual and responds differently to different things. You can try some of the following. Perhaps they will help, but if not, relax and try again later.

- Maybe you've chosen the wrong books where the content is not of interest or the story line too sophisticated. Whatever your child likes doing, whether it's dressing up, cooking, collecting model cars or going to the park, then suggest books that are about similar activities. Let your child choose a book. Even if you don't like it, it's a start.

- Try not to place too much pressure on your child to sit down and listen to you read. Don't try and drag your child away from something he or she enjoys doing. If children are simply counting the moments before they can watch television or go out to play it is unlikely that a book will capture their interest. If you are not getting your child's attention then leave it for another time. You can try reading stories at night just before your child goes to sleep when there are usually fewer distractions.

- Try telling stories to your child rather than reading them. My children love to hear stories about my childhood, especially when something went wrong. It's surprising how similar my childhood adventures and problems are to theirs and to the ones that appear in books, in spite of the generation gap. You can also make up stories and include some of the characters and events that occur in books that are suitable for your child.

- At pre-school or nursery school ask the teacher if your child enjoys book reading time. Say that your child isn't interested in books at home and you may be offered some suggestions on how you can engage your child in a book and the type of book that might be suitable.

No time or energy Work and family life with their endless lists of jobs are both exhausting and time-consuming. No wonder many of us have so little time or energy for reading to our children. It may seem so much easier to leave the whole business of reading to the schools. But don't despair! Most parents have the same problem. Keep in mind that it is not the amount of time that you spend but rather the quality. If either you or your child is exhausted it is definitely best to delay reading until another time. Some ways of coping:

- Try to enlist the help of someone else, such as your wife, husband or an older child. This works in my house. My husband regularly puts our children to bed and reads them a story.

- Remember, quality is more important than quantity. Spending a short time less frequently with your child is much more productive than any number of daily sessions filled with yawns and tension.

- Snatch times when you wouldn't normally think of reading to your child, such as while waiting at the doctor's or dentist's, or any place where you may be held up. Keep a book in your bag for such opportunities.

Some answers to questions

In this section I hope to answer some of your questions that may not have already been answered.

Should I teach my child the alphabet?
I feel that children generally don't need to be taught the alphabet. They learn it anyway by watching 'Sesame Street' on television and from their

alphabet books and friezes. As they get older they begin to see the relationship between the letters in the alphabet song and those that make up words. My daughter, Emma, at the age of two enjoyed pointing to all words that started with 'E' or 'e' as we read stories together. She thought they were the best words, because they began with the first letter of her name.

By all means take advantage of their knowledge of letters and practise the alphabet and the sounds the letters make. Opportunities arise all the time. When driving or walking round the streets your child will begin to notice number plates on cars and signs on the shops. Your child will want to know how to spell his or her name and even the names of other members of the family. Your child may point out letters in a book you are reading and tell you, 'That's a "p"!' proudly. Your child may ask, 'What letter's that?' many times. Many long car and bus trips are rescued from the inevitable 'How far is it to go?' 'Are we nearly there?' questions by games like 'I spy' (You can use the sound of the letter for very young children) or finding number plates that start with the letters in your child's name. Treat these occasions as a game rather than a test.

Should children be taught how to read at pre-school or nursery school?
Pre-schools differ in their policies on teaching reading. Some follow a formal programme, others emphasise 'pre-reading' skills, while still others place more emphasis on socialising skills. There are no hard and fast rules. Just because there isn't a formal teaching programme and just because your child isn't reading independently, even after some time there, doesn't mean your child isn't learning to read. If your child is being read to, has access to books and is getting the idea that printed words mean something, then he or she is, in fact, learning to read.

I would be concerned if there were no books at the nursery school. Talk to the teacher and ask if there is a story reading time. If there isn't and if the books on the bookshelves are untouched, then say something. Meanwhile, if you have time, read to your child and relax with the knowledge that he or she will officially learn to read at 'big' school. Remember, a love of books and stories is the key to learning to read rather than an early formal reading programme.

Will it cause problems if my child learns to read before going to school?
Some parents worry that children who can already read before they go to school may have some difficulties fitting into a class of non-readers at school. However this is rarely a problem. Classes at school have children from a wide range of backgrounds and so there is already a great diversity of knowledge and interest in books, in spoken language and in social development. Teachers are aware of these differences and are trained to cater for them. When your child starts school, tell the teacher the types of books, that he or she can already read and enjoy. The teacher will appreciate this knowledge and will be more able to meet your child's

needs. Besides, there is every chance that there will be other children in the class who are in a similar position.

Should I label the furniture?

This may sound an odd question, but it is one that has been put to me by a number of parents. Some of you feel that you can help your child read by labelling the furniture around the home. I have, in fact, seen several homes with chairs, the ceiling, doors, the carpet and the fridge all labelled. Does it help? I don't think it can do any harm but I feel that there are already many signs and labels in and around the home that convey meaningful messages. For example, the 'Exit' and 'Pull' signs on doors, the 'Ladies' and 'Gents' signs on toilet doors, and the 'Toys' sign in the department store.

The meaning of these signs, like the label 'chair' on a chair, is obvious because of the context. However, real signs and labels have the added advantage that they serve a real purpose. There is a reason for writing 'Pull' on a door and 'Exit' on the way out of a shop or building. So it's better (and simpler!) to use labels and signs that convey 'real' messages. The natural environment has plenty to offer.

I know how important books are but I simply can't afford to buy them. What should I do?

I agree that books are expensive and the problem is that the more you read to your children the more books they need. Use libraries as much as you can. If it is difficult for you to go frequently, talk to the librarian and try to arrange to borrow more books at each visit. You can also arrange a book-swapping system with your child's friends or at pre-school. There are many parents in a similar position who would welcome the opportunity to widen their children's reading resources. I find this works really well for my own children and friends. We lend and borrow books constantly. Also if family and friends ask what your child wants as a birthday or Christmas gift, suggest a book – perhaps a favourite one or one that has caught your child's eye in a bookshop. This is one way of building up your child's personal library.

Chapter Four

Beginning school (5 to 6 years)

Most parents of pre-school children think of themselves as 'bringing up' their children and know that a certain amount of teaching is part of this. But often as their children walk through the school gates they feel they are handing over this 'teaching' role to the school and to the professional teachers. Some parents are relieved to be free of this responsibility, while others would like to continue to take part in their child's education but are not sure what to do. This uncertainty may be reinforced by those schools and teachers who resist non-professional help.

However, I believe that as parents you are well able to help. It is important that you continue to take part in your child's education after he or she begins school. While the school adds an extra dimension to your child's life and has a powerful effect on his or her education, the home continues to have a strong influence. Your child's life in the classroom cannot be separated from what happens outside. In this chapter I hope to provide you with some ways and means by which you can contribute to your child's development as a reader.

Parents of children beginning school are keen that their child should learn to read and fortunately most children do indeed learn. While during these years school is of great importance in the area of reading, home can be just as important. Already by reading, talking and listening to your child and by providing books and other things to read, you have been actively involved in your child learning to read. All these things needn't stop now. Your continued support and encouragement will benefit your child greatly. You can give this by going on reading to and reading with your child, by choosing suitable materials and by working together with the school.

Continuing with reading

Reading to your child   Many parents stop reading to their children once they have started school or when they can read themselves. While most children enjoy this new-found independence we needn't take it as a sign that they are too old or don't need to be read to any more. There are many reasons why you should continue reading to your child even after they have begun school. Here I have noted just a few.

Keeping up the interest in books   Reading to your children helps them become involved in a story and become familiar enough with it to read it alone. It can also encourage them to tackle books that at first appear too difficult. Occasionally both my daughters stop reading because they've read everything at home they feel they can read. I try to take this opportunity to read a different story or a different type of book to them, such as poetry or short stories or even an article in a magazine. Often this helps to widen their reading options. You don't always have to read the whole book to get this effect. Often the first few pages or the first chapter are enough to 'pull' them in, and another way is to read alternate chapters or pages with them.

Widening experiences of books

There is already a wide range of different kinds of books your child can enjoy at this stage. Each type is written in a different way. The differences are not just in content or story line, but in language and appearance. For example, compare the differences between a picture book, a poetry book and an information book. It is a good idea for your child to get to know a variety – and you can help by choosing to read from different kinds of books.

Developing language

The language of children in the early years of school is developing all the time. The stories that you read contribute greatly to this development. Fairy tales, folk tales and many other books that may be too complicated for them to read themselves, are ideal for reading to your children. Both their spoken language and their knowledge of written language expands. Don't be frightened away from books that contain big words or complex language. Your child can understand a lot more than he or she might say or read. The benefits of reading to your child are far-reaching. But of course its success depends so much on *what* you read. This issue is taken up in the next section on picking the best books.

Reading with your child

Reading with your child often happens quite naturally. When reading to children we often find that they are reading along with us. Sometimes our children might even sound like an echo repeating everything we say. Other times they finish a sentence before us. You may feel that they can do this because they are so familiar with the story that they know each word off by heart. However, as your child gets older you will probably notice that this happens even with new stories. It isn't just memory that helps your child finish a sentence. It is probably because he or she is now predicting what is going to happen next from what has already happened. In other words, your child is reading. This should certainly be encouraged. Here are two ways of doing so.

- When reading a story, simply stop every so often and give your child a chance to finish the sentence. This is particularly easy if the story is familiar to your child or if the language is fairly repetitive. Don't try to test your child by asking him or her to tackle words that are too difficult. Remember success and confidence are particularly important at this stage of their learning. The more times your child is right, the more likely it is that he or she will have a go next time.
- Simply read the story as you normally would and encourage your child to read along with you. You can run your finger just under the line, if you wish. Tell your child not to worry about making mistakes or leaving out words,

but just to try to keep up and join in out loud later as the words and the story line become more familiar.

Today there are many stories on tapes with accompanying books that your child can use in a similar way. These are particularly useful when you haven't got the time or the energy to read to or with your child. Your child can listen to the tape, follow the book at the same time and join in as often as he or she likes. The tapes often have the sound of a bell or a musical note which can help your child find the right place. The types of stories recorded on tape are usually familiar to children. This will encourage them to be involved and read along and later perhaps read without the tape.

Choosing suitable books

Children beginning to read need first and foremost plenty of good books that keep their interest in reading going. We hope that these will also extend their experiences and develop their language, as well as their reading skills. Fortunately, there are many good books that can do these things. When choosing books we need to take into account that some are suitable for them to read themselves, while others are more suitable for us to read to them.

For independent reading

As children show signs of becoming independent readers, there is a great temptation to choose books for them that are specifically written for young children learning to read. These books, or 'readers' as they are often called, are usually graded in some way, often so that only a few new words are introduced in each book. Recent reading schemes have become more interesting and imaginative, and some have extensions to cater for children's particular interests and also for home reading with parents. It is my view, however, that these reading scheme 'readers' still don't offer anywhere near the pleasures or advantages of 'real' books. By 'real' books, I mean books that are not written for teaching reading, but just for children to enjoy! They are the books that you have already been reading to your children and the ones that you will, I hope, continue to read to them. It is these books that interest and excite them. Remember we want our children to enjoy reading and we want to make reading easy for them so that they feel successful. I'm not suggesting that these books are never to be found in schools. On the contrary, most schools will have a class library shelf of them, as well as the usual reading scheme readers.

The advantage of real books

Real books offer a huge range and variety of topics and styles. You and your child can choose from poetry books, joke books, books that give them information on science, space, animals, etc., 'how to . . . ' books, story books about happenings in children's own lives, about their dreams and fantasies, their fears and anxieties. In good story books children will recognise their own lives, experiences, language and emotions, feelings and imagination. Good stories tug at your child's feelings, excite and keep their interest. Such books can make them laugh or make them cry.

Real books, unlike readers, do not encourage competition amongst their friends or their brothers and sisters. Reading isn't measured in terms of quantity or book numbers. Your child is able to read a book many times without fearing that he or she is falling behind the rest of the class.

Real books contain natural language. The language isn't manipulated or simplified for a particular reading age. Some of these books have the rhythms of natural speech – the language your child is used to. Some use language that is predictable either because of its rhymes, its repetition or its cumulative lines – books like these are a great help to the beginner reader. Such language can draw your child into the story, which makes reading enjoyable and makes it easier to predict what will come next. It also lifts the book from the boredom of simplified sentences, which sometimes offer nothing other than a string of words. The exaggeration and humour found in natural language are also a welcome attraction.

The illustrations in good picture books are more attractive and alive and vital to the story. If you compare an illustration from a 'real' book with one from a graded reader, you'll see which one excites you and makes you want to read the book. Your child is the same. Also, good illustrations provide important clues to the meaning of the story, which yet again makes reading easier. Your child needs to be able to use the pictures so that he or she can tell what the story is about. A useful hint is to look at the pictures yourself and see if you can follow the story without reading the words.

Some useful books

Below are some books that may be suitable for your beginner reader. There is a fuller list in chapter seven, and many of the books mentioned for three to four year olds are also suitable. Often the books that you read to your child before he or she started school are the favourites and the easiest for reading alone.

When choosing books for your child to read alone, remember that enjoyment and success are what matter most. Take into account first what your child is interested in and knows about. Secondly, try to make sure that the book is roughly at the right level of language so that your child won't too easily get stuck and give up. And, thirdly, have a look at the pictures and judge whether they will appeal or not. Also give your child the chance to choose with you. Often he or she knows best.

Picture books

The Patchwork Quilt by Valerie Flournoy (Bodley Head)
Andy: An Alaskan Tale by Susan Welsh-Smith (Cambridge)
Stories from Our House by Richard Tulloch (Cambridge)
A Baby Sister for Frances; *A Birthday for Frances*; *Bedtime for Frances*; *Bread and Jam for Frances* by Russell Hoban (Puffin/Hippo Books)
Clive eats Alligators by Alison Lester (Oxford)

Although I encourage the use of real books at home, as opposed to books that are specially written for children learning to read, there have been several series of books published that have overcome the problem of simplified stories and language. Some examples are:

Bodley Beginners – Bodley Head
Banana or Champ Books – Heinemann
Read Along Stories – Cambridge University Press

There are many books available in each series and they need to be carefully chosen. While some are just right for some six year olds, others may be too difficult. It depends so much on the individual child. If your child can read them, then fine. However, if they are too difficult then leave them until your child is older; meanwhile read them **to** your child, if they are particularly attractive.

Also, remember that reading needn't be confined to books. The world of print that surrounds your child is growing every day, and as his or her reading skills develop, an awareness of all types of reading materials increases dramatically. Newspapers, TV guides, greeting cards, mail, advertisements, street signs will all have much more meaning. Take advantage of these. Perhaps your child can find his or her favourite television shows in the TV guide, or give the mail to the members of the family, or read a postcard or Christmas card from Gran. Perhaps your child can tell you what a notice from school says or read the ads and signs in the shops. My younger daughter, Kate would read every road sign she could find. She would tell me if I had to stop at an intersection or if I could turn right or if a street was one way. While at times this can be a bit unnerving, it is important to encourage this type of reading. It reinforces the idea that reading is not always done in the same way and it is an easy way to boost children's confidence. Fortunately, perhaps it is only a short-lived stage! Also, try using your child's own stories for reading, as described in chapter three 'Making children's books'.

If reading to your child is a habit already established in pre-school years and if the stories are enjoyable, I'm sure you will meet with little resistance. However, if your child shows little interest, then try another book or try again some other time. Of course, once again, let your child join in with the selection, as this usually does the trick.

Story books   *Babar and the Little Elephant Series* by Jean and Laurent de Brunhoff (Methuen)
Winnie the Pooh; The House at Pooh Corner by A.A. Milne (Methuen)
The Fat Cat by J. Kent (Puffin)
Mrs Pepperpot Series by Alf Proysen (Puffin)
Lion at School and Other Stories by Philippa Pearce (Viking Kestral)

Many of the books mentioned in chapter five are also suitable.

Folk and fairy tales   Children and parents alike may share enjoyment of traditional folk tales and fairy tales. I'm sure many of the tales are already familiar but the following collections offer wonderful interpretations and illustrations.
Legends of the Sun and the Moon collected by Eric and Tessa Hadley

(Cambridge University Press)
Topsy Turvey Tales by Leila Berg (Magnet Books)

Anthologies	The following books offer collections of stories, poems and songs, which are a thoroughly enjoyable source of pleasure for many reading times. *The Puffin Children's Treasury* compiled by Clifton Fadiman (Viking Kestrel) *Tell Me A Tale* by Jean Chapman (Hodder & Stoughton)
Poetry	Poems are often a neglected source of reading and are ideal for reading **to** your child. Within a short space they carry so much meaning and so many feelings. The following collections, as well as all of those mentioned in chapter three, are an exciting mixture of traditional and modern poetry. *Once Upon a Rhyme: 101 Poems for Young Children* edited by Sara and Stephen Corrin (Faber/Puffin) *I Will Build You A House* compiled by Dorothy Butler (Hodder & Stoughton)

Non-fiction materials for five and six year olds

Many five and six year old children enjoy non-fiction books, that is, books that tell them about things. There is quite a large range of suitable books available. Most of them are ideal for reading **to** young children but because they are full of pictures, children are also often able to 'read' the books themselves. As with fiction books, the books you choose will depend a lot on your child's particular interests. Below are just a few of the many books available. Some of the book titles for seven to nine year olds may also be suitable.

How and why things work

Children of this age group often begin to show an interest in the workings of the world. As their world expands so does their curiosity about how things work and why things are as they are. The following titles are a good introduction to this growing interest:
Science Early Learner Books by Bob Graham (The Five Mile Press) – Water; Senses; Heat; Push; Moving; Sound
On the Farm Series by Peggy Heeks and Ralph Whitlick (Wayland) – Autumn on the Farm; Wheat on the Farm; Potatoes on the Farm; Buildings on the Farm, etc.
Australian Season Series by Denise Bart (Hodder & Stoughton) – Spring Days; Summer Days; Autumn Days; Winter Days
Science is Fun Series (Wayland) – Balls and Balloons; Floating and Sinking; Fun with Magnets; Bulbs and Batteries; The Weather; Wind Play, etc.
Natural History Series (Cambridge) – Undersea Homes; Rain Forest Homes; Mountain Homes; Island Homes; Polar Homes; Desert Homes; About Bees and Honey

Animals

Most children are fascinated by animals. They see all kinds of animals on television and at the zoo. The following titles of books, as well as many in the list above, provide them with interesting background information. They deal with topics such as animals in their natural habitats, their young, their eating habits and their life-cycles.

Animals In the Wild Series (John Ferguson) – Hippo; Whale and Dolphin; Penguin; Tiger; Panda; Elephant; Monkey; Kookaburra; Kangaroo; Turtles and Tortoise, etc.

In The Wild Series (Wayland) – Bears in the Wild; Beavers in the Wild; Camels in the Wild; Giraffes in the Wild; Seals and Sea Lions in the Wild; Zebras in the Wild, etc.

Life-Cycle Series by Althea (Longman) – Frogs; Butterflies; Birds; Fish; Swans

Sleeping Animals; *Whose Baby?*; *Whose Footprints?* by Masayuki Yabuuchi (Bodley Head)

Transport   Books about the different forms of transport are a welcome addition to children's matchbox toys and fascination with moving vehicles. I'm always surprised at young children's knowledge on such topics and am grateful for the information the following books provide.

Looking at Transport Series (Wayland) – Looking at Buses; Looking at Cars; Looking at Merchant Ships; Looking at Motorbikes; Looking at Passenger Aircraft; Looking at Submarines; Looking at Trains; Looking at Trucks

Themselves   Just as children's interest in the world around them grows, so does their desire to learn about themselves and about how their bodies work. Titles of some good books include:

In and Out and Round About My World by Stefan Lemke and Marie-Luise Lemke Pricken (Cambridge)

The Five Senses by Maria Ruis, J.M. Parramon and J.J. Puig (Fountain Press) – Touch; Sight; Hearing; Smell; Taste

New experiences   As mentioned before books can help to prepare children for new experiences. By reading about these beforehand we can help to minimise our children's fear of the unknown.

First Experiences Series (Usborne) – Their New Baby, Going to School, Moving House

Visiting the Dentist; *Going to the Doctor*; *When I'm Near Water*; *The New Baby*; *Starting School*; *My Babysitter*; *Moving House*; *Having an Eye Test*; *Having a Hearing Test*; *Going into Hospital*; *A Baby in the Family* and many other titles by Althea (Dinosaur Publications)

Coping with problems   There are also books available that help children cope with particular problems. Just as story books can help children deal with their fears of the dark, the sea, etc., non-fiction books also help children understand their particular problems and see they are not alone. Just a few titles are:

Dinosaur Publications by Althea – Special Care Babies; I Can't Hear Like You; I Have Diabetes; I Can't Talk Like You; I Have Two Homes;

I Have a Sister, My Sister is Deaf by Jeanne Peterson (Harper & Row)

Series   There are several series of publications that offer separate books on a whole range of different topics. Some of the better ones include:
First Library Series (Franklin Watts) – Airliners; At the Doctor; Baby Animals; Comets; Computers; Motorbikes; Robots; Satellites; Trucks, etc.
Starters Series (Macdonald) – Ants; Balloons; Bees; Butterflies; Flowers; Mice; Milk; Rain; Teeth; Trains, etc.

Making things   As children's reading skills develop they can also begin to combine their reading skills with other skills. By following written instructions they are able to make things. The books below are also suitable for older children. At this stage your child may need your guidance.
The Know How Books (Usborne) – Jokes and Tricks; Flying Models; Paper Fun; Print and Paper; Puppets; Spy Craft; Batteries and Magnets; Fishing; Action Games; Action Toys; Flying Models; Experiments; Detection

Working with the school

I have already pointed out the important part the home environment plays in the development of children as readers. This is so for pre-school children and school children alike. Your home and your child's school together can play a crucial role. A working partnership with the school can benefit you, your child, the school and the teachers. The school can provide the direction you are looking for and *you* can provide the support the schools are looking for. This will lead to a greater understanding of each other's needs, which can only benefit your child in terms of reading and in all areas of education.

How to establish contact   As soon as your child starts school it is important that you try to establish contact with the school. This is an important time to exchange all sorts of information. It helps your child settle into the school and opens up channels of communication. If you are not sure how to get in touch with your child's teacher, telephone the school secretary and ask.

During these early weeks introduce yourself to your child's teacher and tell him or her anything that you think is relevant to the school, such as a medical problem or the fact that a second language is spoken at home. Even what may seem trivial things are important to give your child a good start.

There are some things that you might want to ask the teacher, such as his attitude to parent participation. Are you welcome in the classroom? If so, what times are the most suitable? Perhaps you want to know the best time to approach the teacher about questions you might have as the term progresses. Is any regular time set aside to talk to the teacher? Is the school planning parent/teacher interviews?

Perhaps you want to know how you are informed if the teacher has a problem or a question about your child. Is it by letter or by telephone? Perhaps you might be interested in how the school assesses your child's progress. Are there regular formal tests or do they have ongoing informal assessment? Do you receive regular written reports?

Of course you don't have to ask all these questions the first time you meet your child's teacher. Besides, some may not be relevant to you. Also many schools have quite informative letters of welcome for new parents and children and many of your questions may be answered in them. Don't throw these letters away as they may come in handy later. As the term progresses don't be afraid to talk to your child's teacher about how reading is taught in the school and ask how you can give support at home. Find out about borrowing books. Is there a school library? Is there a class library? Can your child borrow weekly or daily? How much choice do children have in their selection of reading materials?

Keeping up a good working relationship with the school

While your first contact is important it is equally necessary to keep up communication with the school. A good home/school relationship is an on-going process. It involves your child, your child's teacher and yourself, and of course works best when all three of you are interested. Some schools provide plenty of opportunities for this continuing contact and encourage you to take part in school life. Each school will have its own ways like parent nights, formal parent/teacher interviews or helping in the classroom. Find out what happens in your school and if you have the time, take advantage of these. However, if your child's school doesn't provide such opportunities or if you just don't have the time, there are other things that you can do as well.

Your interest in what your child is learning is an important first step. Talk to your child about what he or she is doing at school. Don't throw away all those pieces of paper your child brings home from school but get him or her to tell you what they are about. If you don't understand something, or if your child is worried about something that has happened at school, arrange a time to talk to the teacher.

It is also important that your child is confident about his or her teacher and that this teacher has your approval. Therefore if you disagree with how your child is being taught reading, try not to let your child know. Your child can only become confused if he or she is told that the teacher is wrong. However, if you are concerned about it, then by all means talk to the teacher, not as an authority but rather as a concerned parent. If you have questions about your child and you are unable to go to the school, write a letter and try to arrange an appointment to see the teacher.

Some teachers send books home for children to read. Sometimes these books are accompanied by a letter which encourages parents to comment on their child's reading and the suitability of the particular books. Write honestly rather than just what you feel the teacher wants to hear. You can also use these occasions as opportunities to ask your child's teacher any questions you might have about your child's reading.

The work your child brings home provides another opportunity for bridging the gap between home and school. I deal with this in the next chapter as it is usually between the ages of 7 and 9 that school work starts to be done at home.

Coping with difficulties

The first few years at school are often the most relaxed and problem-free. Your child's world has opened up. Learning, being in 'big' school and making many new friends are generally happy experiences. However, problems sometimes arise. In some ways, this may be because we expect so much of our children in their first years at school. We expect them to behave well in class and in the playground, to make new friends and to learn to read and write. It's a lot for a five or six year old. No wonder not all children meet our expectations.

Perhaps your child isn't interested in reading or is showing signs that he or she has reading problems. If this is so and you are not happy with your child's progress in reading, take heart; you are certainly not alone. At five or six years of age, your child is still very young. Many other children (and parents) are in a similar position. I realise that we often hear success stories, like 'My child can read anything!' 'My child is top of the class!' And although these may be true, please remember that most children aren't in this category. We don't often hear parents admit, 'My child hates books.', 'My child doesn't want a book for his birthday, thanks. He just isn't interested.' Not all children like reading and stay up at night devouring every book in sight, not all children learn to read after two years at school and not all children relish books as birthday gifts.

I hope that knowing your child is not alone may help to lessen your fears that he or she is failing or that you have done something wrong. Still, you might want to do something about it; here are a few things that might help.

- Choose books together with your child. Perhaps your child isn't interested in the ones you are reading to him or her or the ones he or she is expected to read alone. Books on topics that interest your child can make all the difference.
- Perhaps the books your child is trying to read alone are too difficult. Remember, children beginning to read need the support of good pictures and predictable language and story. Try something simpler, and read it together with your child.
- Asking your child to read to you is not always a good idea. Perhaps your child doesn't like reading aloud because he or she is concerned about making mistakes. Your child might feel that it is a test to see if he or she can read accurately, and reading aloud can slow down reading which doesn't help in understanding what the story is about.

- Try to encourage reading for meaning. Perhaps your child is concerned with the sounds of the words rather than their meaning. Before you read a book to your child talk about the pictures in the book and what the story might be about. You can encourage your child to do the same before beginning a book.
- Try to spend more time reading to your child. This is probably the most helpful of all things to do.
- Talk to your child's teacher, who might have some suggestions. Your interest will be greatly appreciated.
- Above all, remove pressure from your child and don't pass on your own worries. A relaxed atmosphere is important. You can't force your child to read. However, gentle encouragement can build your child's confidence, which is the key to successful and pleasurable reading.

Problems with the school

All may be well with your child's reading but perhaps the school your child attends is not interested in parental involvement. Although most schools now recognise the importance of involving parents and appreciate its benefits, there are some schools and teachers who still resist it. In some ways this is understandable, as parents' involvement in schools is only recent and it will take a little time before all schools recognise its value. For a long time teachers have been given the total responsibility of teaching reading and this has given rise to a belief that special training is needed to do a good job. If your child's teacher doesn't want you to be involved, then I suppose all you can really do is back off and say that you are available if needed or if a problem needs to be discussed. You can carry on doing the things I have suggested at home and if all is going well with reading, then don't worry.

Most schools have formal parent/teacher interviews, which are for exchanging information about your child's progress at school. Take advantage of these times. If your school doesn't have such meetings then, perhaps together with other parents, approach the head of the school and discuss the possibility of organising one. I hope the question and answer section following will help you to solve other problems that may arise during these early years.

Some answers to questions

Should I discourage different methods from the ones in this book?
It is important not to criticise the methods used by the teacher to your child. This can only be confusing. However, you can say to your child that the teacher's approach is just one way and you can show him or her another way. For example, if your child often stops at a word and starts to sound it out, then you can suggest other ways of dealing with it, such as keep on reading or look for other clues to its meaning that may be found in the

story. Your child will soon discover the methods which work. Also, if your child brings home graded readers which are boring, don't discard them but try to get some fun out of them and supplement them with real books. Also keep in mind that what counts is that your child has a good teacher and not which method is used. If you like your child's teacher, then don't worry.

Why is my child slow to read?
Every child is an individual and therefore learns things at different speeds. There are many children who aren't reading fluently after two or three years at school and it doesn't always mean there is a problem.

Why was my first child reading at an earlier age than the younger one?
It is quite common for first children to learn to read more quickly than their younger brothers and sisters. Parents have more time to spend with their first child and tend to stimulate them and encourage their learning in all areas. They talk to them more and have more time to answer their questions. This early stimulation helps children to learn things quickly. Second and third children, on the other hand, are sometimes left more to their own devices. Older brothers and sisters often give them attention, but this is different from the attention of parents.

Sometimes younger children react against their older brother's or sister's successes, as a result of 'living in their shadow'. This often happens if children go to the same school and the performance of the younger one is always being compared and contrasted with that of the other one. Try to see your child as an individual and not the younger brother or sister of a 'good' reader, even though this is difficult. Build confidence by praising successes in other areas. Read to him or her more often. Make reading an enjoyable experience by not always insisting on reading aloud to you and by helping the child choose enjoyable books and stories.

I remember my own concern when my second child, Kate, wasn't reading by herself as quickly as her older sister. I thought that perhaps she wasn't as bright or perhaps the teacher wasn't as good or perhaps my husband and I didn't read enough to her. Whatever the cause, my fears soon disappeared and even though it took longer, she now reads confidently and enjoys reading, although perhaps not quite as much as her sister.

My child always wants me to read to him. How can I encourage him to read books himself?
Most children who are beginning to read feel more confident about reading a book if it has already been read to them. This is good preparation for their own reading, because it familiarises them with the story and the language in which it is written. Don't worry if you have to read a book several times before your child wants to read it alone. The more confident he or she is the more enjoyable it will be and the easier it will be to read alone. You could try talking with your child about the story and looking through the pictures to give the important familiarity. Perhaps your presence and

attention is what your child is looking for and simply sitting near him may be all he wants. Or it could be that your child is worried about a few 'difficult' words. If so, remind him that it is not always necessary to get every word right and that understanding and enjoying the story is the main aim. You can also try reading together.

My child always reads a book aloud. How can I encourage him to read silently?
Reading silently is a skill that comes as children develop more confidence as readers. Children who are learning to read can't read silently. I remember my own daughter looking at my mouth as I was reading the newspaper and asking how it was possible that I could read without my mouth moving. I pointed out to her all the signs and labels that she was reading (she was five years old at the time) without saying them aloud. She became aware that her father, her sister and her teacher were all reading with mouths closed, something which she shortly afterwards achieved herself. When she reached this stage she realised that when she read silently she could read faster and she didn't worry so much about leaving out words that she didn't know.

   Also many children, especially those who have just started school, often associate the word 'reading' with the times when the teacher either reads aloud to the class or the child reads to the class and/or to the teacher. Talk to your child about why it's sometimes more useful to read aloud and sometimes to read silently. For example, usually a person reads aloud if he or she wants to share something that he or she is reading. However, even then, it is usual to read something silently before you read it out to others.

When do children start reading to themselves?
Most children learning to read enjoy reading aloud to someone, especially if they feel good about reading. Your child may want to share their pleasure of these newly found skills or perhaps want to hear the inevitable, 'Well done!' or 'That's great.' It is only a stage which does pass and you will soon have peace. Meanwhile enjoy the fact that your child is a reader and let him or her know that you are proud of that. Praise doesn't hurt and can do so much good.

Do you think the fact that we speak another language at home will affect my child's reading?
If your child can speak English, as well as the other language, then there should be no problems. Problems with reading in English usually only occur if the child can't speak English at all or if he or she lives in an environment that prevents him or her from understanding the kind of life and background shown in books written in English. Therefore if your child enjoys the same experiences as other children, the second language at home can't hurt. In fact your child's knowledge of another language and culture can help. By telling stories in the other language and reading books in that language you can develop his or her general reading skills in a way

that can only enrich English reading. Let the teacher know that you speak a different language at home as this information is important.

However, if your child starts off by not speaking any English, reading in English will be slower. Knowledge of the spoken language is essential to understanding the printed word. Without this knowledge, your child may be able to say the letters or even words but can't understand them. Therefore, your child will need to learn the spoken form of English at the same time as the written form. This may seem like a difficult task, but don't worry. Children learn quickly. After several months at school most non-English speaking children learn to speak good English. Also, teachers these days have a great deal of experience of children whose first language is not English. In inner city schools it is rare to find a class with only English-speaking children.

When my daughter reads aloud, I notice that she leaves out many words. Does this matter?
I don't think so. She is only doing what we all do. We very rarely read every word and in fact we can understand sentences where some of the words are missing. If your child understands what she is reading then don't correct her. However, her teacher might expect her to read aloud 'accurately' and this might involve some practice. Tell your daughter first to read it as she normally does and when she knows what it is about, she should read it again, this time concentrating on expression and accuracy as well as the meaning.

Chapter Five

Gaining independence (7 to 9 years

As children move through primary school they gain confidence and independence both as individuals and as readers. Children begin to spend more time away from home and rely on their parents less. During this stage many children resist their parents' attention and help. This is often particularly so with reading. While we should respect and encourage their growing independence, our continued interest and support in their reading is still extremely valuable. Reading needn't be seen just as a school-based activity and in this chapter I look at how you can continue to help by choosing books that are likely to appeal to your child (fiction and non-fiction), by listening to your child read and by working together with the school.

Listening to reading

Listening to children read can play an important part in their continued enjoyment and interest in reading.

Many children enjoy reading to parents, especially those who are confident readers. However, if your child doesn't want to or if he or she has reading problems, then it is not always a good idea. If this is the case, leave it and, while this section will still be of interest to you, also read the next section in this chapter on problems that can arise and maybe look back at the section on reading with your child in chapter four.

I believe the value in listening to your child read lies in the shared experience between you and not in the potential 'teaching reading' sessions that it might offer. Your child is likely to enjoy the time together and the interest you are showing. Whenever I have the time I try to listen to Kate, my seven year old daughter, read. We both enjoy the closeness. It gives us an opportunity to talk about events and feelings that arise from the story, and gives me a chance to be part of what she is reading at that time. Also it is a pleasure for me to hear both the joy she is getting from the story and the confidence she is developing as an independent reader. I think that this works well because she feels no pressure to get every word right and because she knows I am interested in the story she is reading, although I sometimes have to pretend a bit, rather than how she reads it.

Reading to your child, reading with your child and listening to your child read are not necessarily separate. Sometimes I read Kate the beginning of a story, then we read some parts together and then Kate takes over, at first aloud and then to herself. As Kate's stories get longer and my time gets shorter, our combined efforts seem to satisfy both of us.

However, of course, everything doesn't always run quite so smoothly. Sometimes Kate doesn't want to read or I don't have the time when she wants me to listen. We try to come to some agreement. Just as I realise that there is no point in forcing her to read, she needs to realise that I can't really listen if I am busy with something else.

At other times the story Kate chooses to read is too difficult and she is always getting stuck at unfamiliar words. She gets fed up and loses heart. When this happens I ask her if she would like me to have a turn reading aloud or if we could change to a different story.

Both of these problems highlight the need for listening to remain enjoyable. If there is tension because either of you is too busy or because the story is too difficult or boring, then there can be little pleasure in reading aloud. Try to keep it as relaxed as possible. You can do this by finding the time that suits both of you, by choosing stories that are not too difficult, by praising your child and by being patient. Patience is extremely important as reading aloud can be difficult, especially when your child is worried about making mistakes.

So what about 'mistakes'? Do they matter, and if they do, should you correct them? While it may be very tempting to correct your child's mistakes, it is certainly not always the best thing to do. There are no hard and fast rules to go by, but it may be helpful to think about what happens when you yourself read aloud and about your own reading 'mistakes' for a start. I think there are two important points to remember.

- Everybody makes mistakes when reading (remember the 'bows' passage in chapter one), and these mistakes are more obvious when we read aloud. Sometimes these mistakes matter, while at other times they don't. Very often when they do matter, such as when we can't make any sense of what we are reading, we correct the mistakes ourselves. We might read on and then go back or we might re-read certain parts.

- Reading aloud is more difficult at certain times. Try to recall the occasions when you have to read something aloud. Usually the times when we are anxious about it are the times when we make the most mistakes. It is when we are concerned with making it sound right, when it is a 'test' situation or when we don't understand what we are reading. On the other hand, it is likely there are times when we don't make many mistakes. This is usually when we are relaxed about it, when we are not frightened about being corrected, when we are familiar with what we are reading and when we are involved in the story rather than reading for the sounds the letters make.

It's best if you correct as few mistakes as possible. Correct only those mistakes which prevent your child from understanding the story (or sentence or paragraph). For example, if your child leaves out words like 'in' or 'the' or reads 'boat' for 'yacht' it doesn't matter. The meaning of the story is probably still there. Most mistakes are like this. However, if your child reads the sentence, 'I'm glad you are such a brave person!' as 'I'm glad that you are such a bad person!' then it is likely that the meaning has been missed. By all means tell your child the correct word but don't make a big issue of it, and always give your child a chance to correct the word. Often by reading a few more words or sentences your child notices that something doesn't make sense and will go back and have another go. The fewer interruptions there are, the easier it is for your child to understand the story and the less pressure he or she is likely to feel.

When reading aloud your child may often be stopping at long or difficult words. Perhaps he or she uses the sound of the first letter to guess the word or tries to sound out the whole word (a difficult task for many words, e.g. 'daughter', 'tear'), or just waits and looks to you for help. Possibly the best help is simply to say what the word is. This way there is hardly any interruption so the story isn't forgotten. You can also suggest that your child reads on and doesn't worry about the word, just as we ourselves do when reading.

When reading aloud the same word can be mispronounced throughout the story. My daughter, Kate, read one of the 'Madeline' stories, saying Mary instead of Madeline the whole way through. Even after correcting her she continued to use Mary. But it didn't matter. Madeline was an unfamiliar name to her and difficult for her to get her tongue round. Kate knew it was a girl's name and instead of baulking each time it appeared, trying to remember what it should sound like, she said it the way she knew and so was able to keep on reading.

If you find it hard to believe that with so many mistakes your child is still understanding what she or he is reading, then at the end of the story or chapter, you should simply ask what it was about. However, don't insist on a perfect account. It is quite difficult to retell a story accurately, with all the details. If you are just looking for assurance that your child has understood the story, then a few sentences that give the main ideas is enough. Also, to help your child understand the story don't just ask him or her to start reading page 10 of a story that you started last week without talking about what happened up to that point. Both of you have probably forgotten.

Working with the school

As your child gains independence and confidence, home and school often become more separate. School is school and home is not school. You may also notice that the early enthusiasm about school, which encouraged the sharing of many school activities and experiences with you, will have probably died down. This doesn't mean, however, that you won't have a part to play. The school/home partnership is still important and even though it may need more effort, your continued involvement with the school will be most valuable not only for you, but also for your child and for the teachers.

There are certain links between home and school that make this involvement possible.

Homework It is during these years that children may begin doing some school work at home. Many primary schools give none at all. Others may ask children to do work connected with their school projects, or it may perhaps be 10 to 15 minutes to be spent reading a book, learning spelling words, practising maths tables or doing maths exercises. Whatever it is, homework can be good for the home/school partnership. It can provide the opportunity for you to get a clearer idea of what your child is learning, how it is taught and suggest ways of contributing to his or her education.

I am not suggesting that you have to sit down with your child as he or she works. That would defeat the whole idea. All the same, knowing what your child is doing and being there to answer questions (if you can!) *is* a good idea. Perhaps your child wants to know where to find information, or wants you to listen to him or her read, wants you to check spelling or needs a suggestion for a drawing. Whatever it is, your interest can make your child feel you care about what goes on at school.

Those of you with children doing projects and other work that requires research will find chapter six helpful.

Letters and notes from the teacher Some schools have newsletters that inform parents of past and future school events. These letters provide an important link between home and school. In some schools, as in the one my eldest daughter goes to, there are frequent newsletters, while in others, as in my youngest child's school, there is a newsletter at most once or twice a term. In both cases the newsletter gives me the chance to know what is going on in the school, which is important for me because I rarely have time to go there myself. These newsletters and the other bits and pieces of notes that they bring home (invariably mixed in with lunch leftovers) provide yet another opportunity for my children to talk to me about school and what's going on there.

During these years, problems may crop up from time to time about which you ought to get in touch with the teacher. The temptation for a busy parent is to hope that these problems will go away of their own accord, but sometimes it's wiser to try to do something about them before they get any worse.

Your child may be finding work at school too difficult, may be worried about an incident in the playground or may have fallen behind the rest of the class because of being absent for a while. Perhaps you are worried that your child isn't reading enough or perhaps you are not sure what books your child should be reading. If you are unable to go to the school, write a letter. But if the problem persists then it is probably best to make personal contact.

Also continue to take advantage of any open days and parent/teacher interviews that may occur during the year. These can give you the chance to see what is going on and to ask any questions. These occasions are 'legitimate' times to be seen at school. Some children are embarrassed by a parent's presence at school, especially when their parents haven't been many times before, but 'official' times seem okay to them. Also it's surprising how quickly children (and parents) lose their embarrassment. The more times you go, the easier it is.

Coping with difficulties

Unfortunately not everything always goes according to plan. Sometimes children don't fulfil our expectations of them as readers and sometimes they don't follow the same reading path as their friends or brothers and sisters. When this happens parents understandably get worried. While it may be reassuring to know that the ideal child is in fact more the exception than the rule, I'm sure a bit of advice won't go astray.

The child who can read but won't

While it may be reassuring to know that your child *can* read, it can still be extremely frustrating if he or she is reluctant to do so. There is no universal answer to the problem. You need to tread lightly and at the same time think positively. You can't force your child to read but at the same time you don't have to accept the fact that your child isn't a reader. You must find a middle ground where you don't exert too much pressure but nevertheless provide direction and support.

There are a lot of different reasons why children don't read. For a start, your child may have too many other things to do. What with other interests and hobbies, sports, playing with friends and so on, there may not be enough hours in the day to fit reading in. Or your child may associate reading only with school, and the last thing he or she wants to do after school and at weekends is school-related work. Your child may not be interested in what he or she is given to read. The stories may be irrelevant to him or her, they may not stir the imagination or tug at feelings. Another reason may be that your child does not feel confident and so is reluctant to do what he or she is bad at. Finally, your child may be rebelling against the pressure placed on him or her to read by parents or older brothers and sisters – the 'bookworms' in the family.

Whatever the cause, it is important that you don't make a big issue of it. This may be easier if you realise that not all children are enthusiastic readers and that a lack of interest in reading is not necessarily a sign of a lack of intelligence. Sad as it may be, you cannot quickly teach your child to understand the value of reading and the pleasures it can give. And of course, the more pressure you place on reading the more quickly it is that your child will respond by refusing to read.

Reading needs to be seen as a pleasure and not as a duty or a punishment. One way of achieving this is by choosing 'reading times' carefully. Don't drag your child away from friends or switch the television off in the middle of a programme in order to read a book. Just as we can't force our children to eat green vegetables when ice-cream is being offered, we can't expect our children to read when their playmates are around. But there are more appropriate times, such as when they complain they are bored and have nothing to do. This can happen when friends are on holidays, or when it is too wet to go outside, when there is nothing on television (or worse still the television is broken) or when they are convalescing after an illness. On these occasions, ask your child to find a book and read it aloud to him or her. This will show how books can turn a boring time into an enjoyable one and at the same time your child will enjoy the special attention.

It is also important that you don't force children to read aloud. This is fine for those who like it, but it can also have a damaging effect on children who are 'reluctant readers'. It may be a reminder of school routine, one which your child mightn't like. It may be that your child doesn't feel confident as a reader and reading aloud will only confirm feelings of failure.

Your child's interest in what he or she is reading is crucial to enjoyment in reading. I believe very strongly that the 'right' reading materials can provide the incentive for converting a reluctant reader into a keen one. By allowing children to choose books they want to read, they are more likely to find the 'right' ones. Even if you feel that the books are too easy, have too many pictures or are just plain boring, don't be discouraging or show your disapproval. Sometimes books chosen by us can be on the wrong topic or can be too difficult. On the other hand they may be too simple and condescending. The stories chosen need to capture your child's attention. The best sort are those that are fast moving, start with a bang, make children laugh and can be finished in one sitting. Books of their favourite TV shows and movies can also be appealing and their friends' approval often provides the incentive needed by many children, also 'joke' books are often irresistible.

There are quite a few choose-your-own-plot adventure books that can capture and keep the interest of many reluctant readers. Sometimes children like to be actively involved in what they are reading and in these books the reader is in charge and decides on the course of events. At various stages the reader has to choose which way the story should go. The books can be read several times, each time with a different outcome. 'Storytrails' published by Cambridge are a good example of this type of book, offering a wide variety of topics. In these books the reader becomes the central character and the plot revolves around their choices.

While children's literature is extremely valuable it isn't the only source of reading materials. Non-fiction books, newspaper articles and magazines still count as reading and there are some children who prefer them. Many adults don't read novels, but still read magazines and newspapers or anything on a topic that interests them. Children are just the same. Newspaper articles and magazines that extend your child's interests and hobbies – whether BMX bikes, cooking or computers – should be encouraged.

The activity books listed in the non-fiction materials section in chapter four are also helpful here. They provide reading for a practical purpose which enables a child to make something.

At the same time, children can be helped to gain an interest in fiction by being read to. I cannot emphasise this point enough. If you have the time, try it. You don't always need to read every page and it's often a good idea to stop your reading at an exciting point in the story so your child has to read on to find out what happens. Again the choice of story is important. Look for books that are exciting and have unexpected twists. Some books are difficult to put down because chapters end at crucial points in the story. And of course, you should talk to your child's teacher about your concerns. Ask about their attitude to reading at school and for any suggestions on what you can do at home to recapture your child's interest in reading. In exchange, tell the teacher what you are doing and together, your chances are greater.

The child who can't read

Understandably you may be concerned if your eight or nine year old child can't read. However, it doesn't necessarily mean that your child has severe learning problems or that they will never be able to read. A common reason children aren't reading by this age is because reading has nothing to offer them. They don't see that it has any purpose. Such children are usually not concerned with making sense out of the story but direct all their energies towards getting the words right. This begins a cycle that is difficult to break. The more they battle with each word, the less they understand. The whole exercise seems pointless, so the less often they try. Why read if you get nothing out of it other than confirmation that you can't read?

To break this cycle, your child needs to know that there is a purpose to reading and needs to develop a sense of personal worth so that they have the confidence to do it. It may sound difficult, but it doesn't all rest in your hands. Your child's teacher is no doubt aware of the problem and will be helping your child. By working together a lot can be achieved. Show your concern to the teacher and talk about the different things you are trying at home and ask for any more suggestions. It is important to maintain contact so that while you are working towards a common goal your methods complement rather than contradict each other.

So that your child can regain confidence, it is important not to show your fears that he or she will never be able to read. Your child needs to believe in him- or herself and this will be well nigh impossible if there is a suspicion that you don't. Your child needs confidence and not another reminder that he or she is a failure.

Because reading activities need to make children feel successful it is best to avoid reading aloud to you. Your child's hesitations and mistakes are all the more evident when reading aloud. Anxieties about making mistakes are likely to create more mistakes, which once again reinforce negative feelings. Besides, reading aloud often makes comprehension more difficult. How can your child remember the beginning of a sentence, let alone the beginning of the story, when they are struggling to make each word sound right?

Try to find the time to read to your child regularly. This way your child can become familiar with the language and story lines of books, as well as experience the pleasures and excitements that good books can give. Children need to feel that reading is worthwhile. Having a good laugh, reading about experiences and feelings similar to their own situation, learning about something new, can all make reading worth the effort. Therefore it is essential that the stories are relevant. Don't be concerned about the language or the size of the print. Your main concern at this stage should be that your child enjoys the book and not whether the print is too small or the language too complex for your non-reader. Your child's interests and experiences are the same as any other seven to nine year old and the stories you read need to reflect this. At the same time, don't be frightened away from picture books. Certainly those that are suitable only for young children would be inappropriate but there are now many available that are relevant for this age group and the pictures alone can often draw an uninterested child into a story.

If your child doesn't want to listen to you when you read, you may first need to talk about the story line, using the title and the pictures as cues. This can help get your child involved in the story, so that he or she will want to find out what actually happens.

Sometimes just the mere mention of a book causes immediate tension. If this is so, it is best to leave the story reading for another time or perhaps you can get someone other than yourself to try it. Often parents are so keen that their child should learn to read that the slightest resistance causes anxiety. This may not happen if another member of the family, such as a grandparent, aunt or older brother and sister, has a go.

If your child wants to, he or she can read along with you. This way you are providing a good reading model and your child can see and hear that reading isn't necessarily a word for word accurate process. By following and saying the words with you, your child can hear that you too make mistakes, that you hesitate at times and that you need to reread certain parts in order to understand what you are reading. As your child develops confidence, give him or her the opportunity to finish some of the sentences. This is easiest if the story is familiar and the words are very predictable – perhaps they rhyme or the outcome is obvious.

Another way of persuading your child away from the idea that every word has to be right is to use print other than in books. It is often here that your child can understand that meaning is more important than the sound. It is likely that your child is reading quite a lot of the print without being aware of it. Some examples might be television programmes, television and newspaper advertisements, titles of videos and movies, games, such as Monopoly and Cluedo, instructions for puzzles. All of these types of reading materials reinforce the idea that the print gives a message and that the message doesn't depend on sounding out every letter or every word.

Write stories together with your child as suggested in chapter three. This can also help develop your child's confidence as a reader and encourage the idea that written words have meaning. Initially it is a good idea for you to write what your child says. As tempting as it may be, try not to correct the language while you write. In this exercise it is important that your child is able to predict what words are written down and if they are altered or are not part of his or her own language the task becomes more difficult. The story your child wants to tell should be their own choice, although your suggestions may be helpful. You could suggest a diary type story, with the help of photos perhaps, where your child relates the happenings of a particular day. Perhaps your child may like to retell the events of a particular television programme or movie. If a complete story seems too difficult you can also suggest writing messages to each other. However, if your child is reluctant to do this activity it is best to leave it and not force the issue.

Choosing suitable books

Choosing books for children that will encourage their reading is every bit as important now as it was in the early stages. Added to this, now's the chance to start to feed their increasing curiosity about the world around them through simple non-fiction books.

Fiction
Fiction books suitable for seven to nine year olds can take into account their increasing concentration span and their ability to read silently. Both of these allow them to read books that are longer, and books that have fewer pictures and more words. The picture books of their beginner reading days can now be supplemented with longer and more difficult picture books. You can also choose books that contain perhaps several short stories with quite a few pictures. At this age, children can begin to cope with books that have chapters, first with books where the chapters are completely self-contained (each can be read as a short story), and then leading on to books where the chapters are linked and need to be read in a certain order.

Your child will probably still enjoy many of the topics found in their earlier books, such as family and school stories, animal tales and stories about witches and magic. These topics can now be expanded. They can take into account children's thirst for knowledge, their developing imagination, their increased sense of humour, their need to be reassured that their fears and anxieties are 'normal', and their developing sense of what's right and what's fair and that good should triumph over evil.

At this stage children are likely to enjoy reading different types of stories.

- real stories about friendships at school, such as making and losing friends
- magic and fantasy stories which can relate to their own imaginative 'let's pretend' games
- fairy tales, folk tales, myths and legends, where their sense of morality is confirmed and where they can explore at a distance the cruel realities of life as they sometimes see it

- stories which make them laugh, such as where something goes wrong in their everyday life and where familiar stories and fairy tales are altered in an unexpected way
- stories based on their favourite television series and movies

The following list of suitable books takes into account your children's increased reading ability and interest areas.

Picture books	*The Giraffe, the Pelly and Me* by Roald Dahl (Bodley Head) *The Tram to Bondi Beach* by Libby Hathorne (Methuen) *The Visitors Who Came to Stay* by Analena McAfee (Hamish Hamilton) *Dear Daddy* by Philippe Dupasquier (Puffin/Penguin) *Ming Lo Moves the Mountain* by Arnold Lobel (Julia MacRae) *The Story Of the Dancing Frog* by Quentin Blake (Picture Lions/Armada) *Edward Wilkins and his friend Gwendaline* by Barbara Bolton (Angus & Robertson)
Short stories with pictures	*The Magic Finger*; *The Twits*; *Fantastic Mr Fox* by Roald Dahl (Puffin) *Flat Stanley* by Jeff Brown (Methuen) *Stories from Our House* by Richard Tulloch (Cambridge) *Banana or Champ Books* published by Heinemann *Thing* by Robin Klein (Oxford)
Books with several different short stories	*Revolting Rhymes* by Roald Dahl (Puffin) *A Necklace of Raindrops*; *The Last Slice of Rainbow and Other Stories* by Joan Aiken (Jonathan Cape)
Series	In the following books the characters and the setting remain the same throughout the books, yet each chapter can be read individually. *My Naughty Little Sister Series* by Dorothy Edwards (Methuen/Magnet) *Ramona Series* by Beverly Cleary (Puffin/Hamish Hamilton) Many children enjoy reading books that are in a series. Series books provide the security and familiarity many children need. Not only are they already familiar with the characters and the type of story, but they also know that when they finish one book, another one is just around the corner. Ramona in the *Ramona Series* became part of our family for a while. I was almost pleased when Ramona left the house but I am often reminded of her, especially when I cook with paprika (or 'red stuff', as Ramona calls it).
Books with a continuing story	*The Witch of Monopoly Manor* by Margaret Stuart Barry (Picture Lions) *The Village Dinosaur* by Phyllis Arkle (Puffin) *Follow That Bus*; *The House That Sailed Away*; *The Curse of the Egyptian Mummy*; *The Mona Lisa Mystery* by Pat Hutchins (Picture Lions) *The Worst Witch Series* by Jill Murphy (Puffin) *George's Marvellous Medicine*; *Charlie and the Chocolate Factory*; *The Witches*; *The BFG* by Roald Dahl (Puffin) *Going Bananas* by Max Dann (Oxford) *Penny Pollard Series* by Robin Klein (Oxford)

Poetry   Poems are always a welcome addition to your child's reading. Their humour, their brevity and the pictures they create can be so inviting.
Please Mrs Butler by Allan Ahlberg (Puffin)
Revolting Rhymes; *Dirty Beasts* by Roald Dahl (Puffin)
A First Australian Poetry Book compiled by June Factor (Oxford)
Poems for Nine Year Olds and Under chosen by Kit Wright (Kestrel)
Someone is Flying Balloons compiled by Heylen and Jellett (Omnibus/ Cambridge)

When choosing fiction books of course the first priority should still be books that interest your child, so it is important that he or she has a say. Reading skills are still developing and so don't worry if your child prefers to read picture books. Many children, particularly seven to eight year olds, still need the extra clues that pictures provide. There are also many children who read picture books simply because they enjoy them, even though their reading skills may be good enough to cope with more difficult books. The translation from picture books to stories without pictures may be either quick or slow. Your child is usually the one who knows which type of books he or she can best manage. However, you can also encourage your child to branch out into different types of books. You can do this when you read to your child. My seven year old daughter didn't have the confidence to deal with books without pictures or books that were long. She felt that she had to get through a whole book in one sitting, even though she had seen her sister mark the place when she stopped reading. She felt it was all right to leave stories unfinished when I read them to her but not so if she was reading on her own. At story reading time (bedtime in our house), I slowly encouraged her to read different types of books. It took a while. First I read books with fewer pictures and more words, then when she felt confident to read some of these alone, we moved to short stories. After that we read longer books that were divided into manageable chapters. With each type and at each sitting she or I read part of it, then marked the spot and left it until the next night to continue. Before we started again we discussed what had happened up to that point and then read on. After a while she developed enough confidence to tackle a new book herself and she now enjoys the challenge but still returns to her picture books 'for a quick read'.

Non-fiction   Children in this age group are very interested in what goes on around them. They seem to have endless questions about the world and about the lives of others. Some of these questions are answered by their teachers or by television programmes but their curiosity is never really satisfied. I'm always having to search my mind (and books, if necessary) to try and answer my children's why, when, who, how, what about, what if . . . questions. No wonder we often resort to answers like, 'Ask your father/ mother/teacher!' or simply, 'I don't know.' So many things that we as adults take for granted are a source of intrigue for our children.

Also many children in this age bracket are developing their own interests and hobbies. It might be something practical like gardening, cooking or making their own forms of transport, such as billy carts or skate-boards. It might be an interest in something, such as the universe, guinea pig breeding, goldfish or dinosaurs, that has been sparked off by the current project at school. Whatever it is, unless we have the same interest in the subject, our knowledge is often found wanting.

Fortunately today there are many books and magazines suitable for children that can extend their knowledge and satisfy their curiosity. Of course you still need to be selective as not all are suitable. It is important to check the way a book or magazine is written and the amount of knowledge assumed. Some adult non-fiction books and magazines assume a lot of background knowledge or provide too much information, while those written for children are sometimes oversimplified or contain too little information.

As a parent you can help your child develop their hobbies and curiosity about the world, and at the same time gain research skills that will be needed in later years. By helping your child find the right books, and then the information *in* these books, and by talking to him or her about the topic you can help to satisfy your child's thirst for knowledge. (You might sometimes learn something yourself!)

Helping your child find
the right books

The right books will naturally depend on the topic, the amount of detail needed and the reading ability of your child.

Encyclopaedias come to everyone's mind when talking about non-fiction books for children. You have to be clear for a start which kind you are thinking of. There is on the one hand the large scale alphabetical encyclopaedia in many volumes (modelled on adult ones) such as the Children's Britannica. These cost a good deal but can be excellent sources of information if children are helped to use them so that they do not find the sheer amount of information too daunting. Children need quite a bit of guidance to find the right volume and the right page and to sift through information to find the bit they want. On the other hand there are the shorter single or two-volume encyclopaedias, some alphabetical but more likely to be organised by topic. Although they contain information on a very wide range of topics and can provide excellent material for browsing, they may not contain enough detail to satisfy the young researcher. Broadly speaking, the topic-based approach is better for the younger and the alphabetical for the older user.

If you want to buy an encyclopaedia for the home, try to spend some time choosing it. Look for one that has frequent updates, good and instructive illustrations, an easy to follow index and a clear layout. Also be sure the language is not too complicated. The 1985 Good Book Guide to Children's Books (Penguin) has a detailed survey of children's encyclopaedias. In any case libraries have quite a range of different ones, so don't be too concerned if you can't afford one.

For children who have lots of 'how' and 'why' questions there are many books that are set out in question and answer form. For example: *Dragon Question Books* by Kathie Billingslea Smith (Granada) contain delightfully illustrated answers to the many where, when, why, what, how and who questions that my seven year old asks. There are many others that give more detailed answers on a wide range of topics, such as the *Tell Me Why Series* by Arkady Leokum (Hamlyn). If your child needs more detailed information on a particular topic there will be many books available. When choosing these, make sure they are suitable (that is, neither too advanced nor too simple) by looking at the language, the illustrations and the layout.

There are also quite a few scientific, natural history and geographic magazines for children. Some are excellent but again you need to be selective. Try to check each one in a newsagent, before thinking of signing up for a year's subscription. They are also available for loan in some school and local libraries, so check these too.

Of course, it would be quite unreasonable to expect parents to have a complete reference book collection for their children at home. Apart from the cost, children's interests and knowledge areas are always changing. Try to use your local library as much as you can, swap books with friends or ask relatives if they have any books that their children have outgrown. However, as with fiction books, try to buy a few, so that there are always some on hand. Choose those that are likely to keep pace with your child's interests for a few years. One reference book that is in constant use in our house is our atlas. Good atlases can be wonderful sources of information. *The Macquarie Illustrated World Atlas* has provided a lot of information for many school projects for my children (projects ranging from the universe to the provinces in Canada to a comparison of flags throughout the world). *The Guinness Book of Records* has also provided great amusement as well as interesting facts and fortunately has to some extent taken over as the question and answerer in our home.

Finding the right book is only one step towards finding the information. Often children need help finding their way around non-fiction books.

- Don't feel that you are intruding into the school area by showing your child how to use an index and the contents page, and how headings, sub-headings, **bold** or *italic* print and underlined sections can all help to direct him or her to the relevant information.
- You can give your child practice using an index in a newspaper or show how you find the television programmes, the classified ads, etc. using the index and your knowledge of alphabetical order.
- You can show your child how information on one topic is not always confined to one heading. For example, information about dinosaurs may be found under dinosaurs, under prehistoric animals or under stegosaurus etc.
- You can show your child how the illustrations give them a lot of information.
- You can show that it isn't always important, or desirable, to read every word and there are certain parts, such as the sub-headings and the bold print, that can point to the information the user is looking for.

I know this may sound time-consuming but in the long run it can save a lot of time (yours and your child's) and is well worth the trouble. You can also help by talking to your child about the topic. This can help your child recall things he or she already knows, which can make the reading task easier and clarify the information. For example, if your child needs to find some information on dinosaurs (yet again) you could mention a previous visit to the museum or a TV programme on dinosaurs.

For more detailed information on how you can help your child use non-fiction materials see the section in chapter six.

Most of the non-fiction books listed in the five to six year old section are suitable for this age group but now most children will be able to read a lot of them by themselves. The titles in the five to six year old section can be added to, by taking into account the increasing interests and reading skills that children are now developing. They can now cope with more details and their interest range is broader, as their hobbies start and as school projects begin.

There are many series published that deal with a very wide range of topics –

Exploration and Discovery Series (Macmillan) – Man and the Moon; The Solar System; The Undersea World; The Changing Earth; Lasers and Holograms, etc.

Topics Series (Wayland) – Peoples of the World; Robots; Energy; Costumes and Clothes; Inventions; Jungles; Shops; Television, etc.

Finding Out About Series (Usborne) – Our Earth, Sun, Moon and Planets; Rockets and Spaceflight; Things That Go; Things at Home; Things Outdoors; Everyday Things

First Look At Series (Franklin Watts) – Airports; Arms and Armour; Cats; Computers; Earthquakes; Fossils; Lasers; Prehistoric Mammals; Rocks and Minerals; Volcanoes; Weather, etc.

My First Library Series (Macdonald) – Hearing; Communication; Farms; Air Travel; Homes Around the World, etc.

The Living World Series (Walker Books) – Grasslands; Deserts; Mountains; Jungles

The following books have been divided into school subjects and topics. Many more titles can be found in the ten years and onwards section.

History *The Everyday Life of a . . . Series* edited by Giovanni Caselli (Macdonald) – A Greek Potter; An Ice Age Hunter; A Celtic Farmer; An Egyptian Craftsman; A Viking Settler; A Medieval Monk
Althea's History Series (Dinosaur) – Blood and Thunder; Tricks and Treats; Investigator's Notebook by Josie Karavasil

Computers *Discovering Computers Series* (Wayland) – Computers in Action; Living with the Microchip; The Micro; What Are Computers?

Other people *My Belief Series* (Franklin Watts) – I am a Hindu; I am a Muslim; I am a Catholic; I am a Sikh, etc.

Transport *Looking at Transport Series* by Cliff Lines (Wayland) – Looking at Buses; Cars; Merchant Ships; Motorbikes; Passenger Aircraft; Submarines; Trains; Trucks

Geography	*The Bodley Head Young Geographers Series* (Bodley Head) – Deserts; Making Maps; Polar Lands; Islands; Rainforests; Rivers; Soils and Plants; Weather *Young Explorer Series* (Wayland) – Around the Coast; Climate and Weather; Farms and Farming; Hills and Mountains, etc.
Learning about themselves	*All About You Series* (Wayland) – Your Eyes; Your Hands and Feet; Your Health; Your Nose and Ears; Your Skin and Hair; Your Teeth *You and Your Body Series* (Wayland) – How You Grow and Change; The Structure of Your Body; Your Body Fuel; Your Brain and Nervous System; Your Heart and Lungs; Your Senses
Science	*Simply Science* (Franklin Watts) – Atoms; Climate; Electricity and Magnetism; Everyday Chemicals; Forces In Action; Sound and Music; Water, etc. *Space Scientist Series* (Franklin Watts) – Comets and Meteors; The Moon; The Planets; Quasars and Galaxies; Stars; Sun *Simple Science: How Things Work* by Martyn Bramwell and David Mostyn (Usborne)

Some answers to questions

What is dyslexia? Do all children who can't read suffer from dyslexia?
Dyslexia is a term often used to describe children who have reading difficulties. It implies that there is a physiological or medical reason for a child not being able to read. While in some cases this may be true, the term is generally misused and leads to the idea that a child with reading difficulties needs to be 'cured', which is only possible with special 'treatment'. Often children who write their 'b's' and 'd's' backwards, who write 'saw' as 'was' and who can't blend 'b' and 'l' together to make the 'bl' sound are called dyslexic. Yet all of these are common in many beginner readers (and writers) and certainly do not always indicate a learning disorder.

I don't believe that all children who can't read have dyslexia and I feel it is best not to look for a medical reason for children's reading difficulties or for a special cure. More often the most beneficial things to do are to make reading a pleasurable activity, to read to your child and to believe that your child will learn to read.

Is it true that girls like reading more than boys?
Many people believe that reading is more popular with girls than with boys of this age group. On the whole this seems to be true but I'm sure we could all find families where a son reads more than the daughter and where an older sister reads more than a younger sister. Individual differences as well

as differences in sex affect our children's reading habits. I don't think that girls are born to enjoy reading more, but I do think that our society's expectations of what girls and boys should like influence what they read and the amount of time they spend reading. It is said that boys prefer to be more active and are influenced by their friends who often regard reading as 'sissy'. It is also said that the books that are available for this age group are more directed towards girls' interests. Whatever the cause I don't think that you have to accept that your sons will read less than your daughters, because such expectations can influence the outcome.

My child always reads books with pictures in them. Is this really reading?
Yes, it is really reading. Young readers need the support of pictures to help them predict what a story is about and to give meaning to what they are reading. Reading should be an enjoyable experience and should be made easy for young readers. It is neither of these if a child has to read the words without first having any idea what they will be about. Pictures, on the other hand, allow children to tap into their knowledge and experiences that are relevant to the particular book. This knowledge enables them to predict the story and enjoy it as well. The popularity of picture books is not just confined to beginner readers. Many experienced readers, including adults, can gain a lot of pleasure from them. Good pictures complement and extend the written language and because they give vital clues to the meaning of the story, they should be taken advantage of rather than discouraged.

The words 'oral reading', 'reading comprehension', 'word attack skills', and 'blends', all appear on my child's school report, under the heading of reading. What do they mean?
Some schools divide reading into a number of skills.

Oral reading usually refers to the child's expression when reading a passage or story aloud. Previously it was seen to be synonymous with reading but it is now understood that a person can read a passage fluently and with good expression without necessarily understanding it and vice versa. Reading aloud can be an important skill, but it is a different skill to reading for understanding. In fact, concern with good expression often interferes with comprehension.

Reading comprehension refers to the child's ability to understand what he or she is reading. This is assessed in different ways and might include:
- An oral or written retelling of a story, which the child has just read.
- Answering comprehension questions in writing after reading the passage or story.
- Completing a cloze. A cloze is a passage in which certain words have been left out and the child must fill in these spaces so that the passage makes sense.

Word attack skills refers to the child's ability to use the different clues available to recognise and understand a 'difficult' word. These clues include the letters, which help work out the sound of the word. The child sounds out each letter or uses the first letter of the word to prompt his or her recognition. They also include the contextual clues, which help work out the meaning of the word. These may be pictures or the words or sentences before and after the word which give the word the meaning.

Blends refers to the child's ability to blend together the sounds of a word to form the whole word. For example, 'd-o-g' blends into 'dog' and 'st-op' blends into 'stop'. However, it is impossible to sound out and blend all words. We would have to learn 166 phonic rules in English and 661 exceptions to do it successfully.

My daughter is eight years old and I am told she has a reading age of six. What does this mean?
The concept of a reading age was developed to tell teachers and parents how children are reading in relation to other children of the same age. However, it is not necessarily accurate. The assessment is generally based on the performance on one particular test and assumes that all children of a certain age have had similar experiences and have similar knowledge.

The results of these tests should be no cause for alarm. These tests cannot predict how well your child will be able to read in the future and can only do harm if your child hears that her reading age is lower than the others in the class. You are the best measure of your child's reading ability. If she enjoys reading and reads regularly then don't worry. If, however, she never reads at home and appears to avoid reading then talk to her teacher, read to her more often and encourage her to choose her own books.

My child is eight years old and has a reading age of twelve. Should he be reading books for twelve year olds?
Not necessarily. As pointed out in the answer to the previous question, a reading age is not necessarily a good way of telling what your child is able to read. It tells you how your child has performed on a certain battery of tests. Deciding what is the right kind of reading depends on many other factors, such as what your child knows already about the subject, whether he or she is familiar with that kind of language and that kind of book. For example, an eight year old would have trouble understanding a book about adolescent experiences, no matter what his or her 'reading age' was. There is an enormous range of suitable books, written for the whole range of interests and needs of eight year olds, so take advantage of these.

My child never seems to remember what he has read. When I ask him to tell me what a book is about he says he's forgotten. How can I improve his memory?
I don't think this is a memory problem. Most open-ended questions asked of children meet with similar responses. How often do you ask your child, 'What did you do at school today?' and the response is, 'I can't remember,' or 'Nothing.' It isn't that he has really forgotten. It may be that he wants to be left alone, or that he feels you don't really want to know or perhaps he doesn't have enough information to build on and needs a question that is

more specific. The same is true when asking children about the books they have read. You can try and be more specific in your questions, but also ask yourself *why* you are questioning your child about a book. Often children feel anxious about being questioned on what they have read. They get enough of that at school. Leave the comprehension questions and story analysis to the classroom and let your child enjoy books at home without worrying about an interrogation.

If my child's teacher can't help him, how can I?
Many parents feel that because teachers are 'the experts', they are the ones with the most tricks up their sleeves to help children read. Therefore if children can't read, or don't like reading, then there is little that parents can do to alter the situation. This belief is based on the idea that reading needs to be taught by 'professionals' and is a skill that is unrelated to children's lives, homes and knowledge of language.

However, as I've pointed out many times, this is not the case. Your child's background and experiences are crucial, firstly to their understanding of what they are reading and secondly to their enthusiasm, or lack of it, for reading. You, as a parent, have contributed greatly to these experiences and your understanding of your child's interests and needs can certainly help. You can provide the individual attention so often lacking in classes of 25 to 30 children. The interruptions of the class and the demands of other children do not lend themselves to an ideal learning situation for a child who needs special attention. You can choose books with your child that are absolutely right for his or her own interests and needs, you can read to your child and talk about the story or relevant experiences and you can listen to your child read without the interruptions of the normal classroom.

Armed with the knowledge and ideas gained from this book and from your understanding of your child's needs you can, indeed, make a valuable contribution to your child's acquisition and enjoyment of reading.

Chapter Six

Developing reading (10 years onward

Most children by the time they are ten years old are competent readers. For some this means that their reading has opened up and they now read everything they can lay their hands on. While this is true for many, often as children approach adolescence they lose their enthusiasm for reading and move away from reading for pleasure. This change is often a result of the increased demands of school work, the amount of time taken up by their social life, hobbies and interests, and the fact that reading is no longer seen by their age group as the sort of thing you ought to be doing. However, despite all this, children should be encouraged to keep on reading for pleasure and fun. Children's literature can play an important part in their social and intellectual development.

Without needing special skills or having to spend hours each evening with your child you can help your child through this period. In the following sections I will suggest how you can help your child read non-fiction materials, increase his or her understanding of what is read and extend the range of fiction books.

Reading non-fiction

At this stage a lot of children's school work involves finding out information – what is called 'research' in schools – for projects. It is in this area where, to my mind, you can help most.

What is research? Research, in the very simplest form, is gathering information about a topic. While some children are used to finding out about things in the course of their daily lives (such as gathering information about their favourite rock group or using the newspaper to find the costs of second-hand bikes), there are many who aren't. However, at school, all children need to do 'research' of this kind. They might need to find out the background of an author or the life cycle of a particular insect. It might be to find out about the beginnings of space travel or about animal life in the Antarctic. The topics will vary but the research skills remain similar.

There are three elements to research:

- knowing and understanding your purpose, that is, what your topic is and what you need to know
- finding the information
- understanding the information

In this section I look at how you can help your child develop the skills for finding the books he or she needs and then for finding the information in these books.

Perhaps you feel uneasy about helping. You may think it's up to your child to learn how to complete a task. In the following suggestions, your child will still be doing the work, but you will be providing guidance. Projects involving some work out of school are not tests, but are intended to develop and practise certain skills, such as researching, writing and presentation. These skills cannot be learnt overnight and they will be needed all through school.

Some of the points covered may seem very simple, but to many children they won't be. Although your child may be perfectly at home reading fiction, reading for information, using non-fiction books, is another matter. You may be lucky and it may be something that is actually taught at your child's school (as part of 'study skills'), but often children are left to pick this up for themselves, and when they have to prepare at home for, say, a project, they get bogged down and easily discouraged.

Preparation

When your child has been given a particular task to find out about something, it is helpful if you first discuss the topic with him or her. You will need to know:

- what has to be done
- what your child already knows about the topic
- what the teacher has told the class about it
- what has to be found out

This will give your child a chance to start talking about the topic and (perhaps with a bit of help from you) using the words and terms connected with it.

Ask your child if the teacher has made any suggestions about suitable reference books. If you haven't got these books at home or they aren't available at school, try your local library. Librarians are usually helpful and will show your child how to use the catalogue and how to find the books on the shelf. It may be worthwhile for you to go through the process of finding the books together (using the index and finding the reference number etc.), just to show how it is done. The main thing is to get your child to find the right section and to start browsing.

It will help your child to know that the information needed is not always found in one book. Several books may have to be used. Even so, don't get too enthusiastic as children sometimes find it a bit daunting if you take too many books from the shelf. It may also be worthwhile pointing out to the older child that 'facts' on the same subject are not always the same in different books. People writing books – or anything else – write in different ways and have different views on a subject. A good way to show this is to have your child compare two snippets from different newspapers on the same subject. Almost always, facts have been added or left out and the emphasis is different.

Encourage your child to try to get an idea of the level of a book before plunging in, so that he or she is not put off by language that is far too difficult or assumes too much background knowledge. If your child has used similar reference books before and is familiar with the way they work, then all the better. However, don't get stuck on always using one type, such as encyclopaedias.

Finding the information

This involves the use of a range of different ways of reading: looking things up, skimming, scanning and reading in detail. These skills are, of course, used by all readers at different times. Children need to see that finding information for their interests and everyday needs and reading to find information for their learning at school are very similar.

Children have got to learn that *how* we read at any one time depends on *what* it is we are reading, *why* we are reading it and *what we know* about it already. They need to see that they don't need to read every word to decide if a book is useful or to find the information they want. For example, when looking up a telephone number you wouldn't dream of reading every word in the telephone directory, yet you may need to read every word of the instructions for a new kitchen gadget. The same applies to school work. Children may sometimes need to find specific information, such as a date or a name of a person or town, while at other times they might need to read a whole section slowly and carefully, in order to take in a lot of the detail.

Looking things up

In modern life everyone needs to be able to look up information organised in some sort of system, such as alphabetic or numerical order, as, for example, looking up a telephone number, looking for a street in a street directory, looking up a word in a dictionary and using an index in the newspaper to find the classified ads. We learn how to do this by practising what are called in school 'reference skills'.

We use these same 'reference skills' when looking for a book in a library and then finding the information in the book. For example, if your child needed to find some information on the life of people in the province of Quebec, Canada, you might look together under 'Q' for Quebec or 'C' for Canada to find the right reference numbers in the catalogue. You'd be likely to find quite a few books catalogued under those numbers and together you would have to make up your minds which might be the most useful. After finding the right shelf you would show your child how to use the contents page at the front of a book and the index at the back using alphabetical order. The information needed for the Quebec project would probably be under different headings such as people, climate, food, languages, cities, industries, farming, sport and leisure activities.

Skimming

Skimming is quickly looking through a page, a chapter or a whole book to get a general idea of what it's about. It is what we do when looking for something to interest us in a newspaper or a magazine, when looking for a book to buy in a bookshop or when re-reading something we are familiar with. You may need to skim several articles or chapters in order to find something useful. The headings, sub-headings, anything written in bold print, drawings, diagrams and photographs, the first and last sentences, can all give clues. Remember it is important to stress that you shouldn't read every word. It would take far too much time, time wasted if that particular piece were not what you wanted. That's one of the purposes of skimming – to help you decide whether or not something is worth reading in detail.

Scanning   We scan something when looking for specific information, such as when looking up the entertainment guide to see what time a film starts, when checking a doctor's appointment card for the time, when reading the weather report to find out what the temperature will be, when looking for the amount due on your electricity bill. We pick out only the information we need and ignore the rest.

In the Quebec research a child might first scan the contents page of a book to see if it contains any information on life in Quebec. After finding the relevant chapter or pages he or she might then scan the section giving the total population of the province, the population of Montreal, the average temperatures in winter and summer or the average rainfall, etc. If you are clear what you are looking for then scanning for specific information can save a lot of time.

Reading in detail   We read carefully and slowly in order to get the full meaning out of something. We might read a legal document in detail, an interesting newspaper article or a letter from a friend. Usually we skim the text first to get a general idea. We may then find it necessary to read it in more detail, depending on our purpose in the first place. At this stage it is important that your child knows that materials can be read in all sorts of different ways and it is only necessary to read some things in detail. For example, again back to the Quebec project, your child probably wouldn't read in detail an article or chapter on the political situation or the stock exchange, as it would not fit that particular project. However, articles about the climate, bi-lingualism, sporting activities, housing and food *would* be of interest in a project on the life of people in Quebec, so perhaps some or all of these would be read in detail.

Increasing understanding

Children in upper primary and secondary school years have to read and use many different types of books. They have to read stories and poems in their English lesson as well as lots of factual books for other subjects. They often have to use the knowledge gained from that reading to answer questions and write about topics. Children are sometimes bewildered by the sheer volume of reading they are asked to do. At the same time, parents worry whether their children are understanding everything that they read.

Some things are easy to understand. When the reader knows why he or she is reading something, or chooses to read it of their own free will – that's a good start. Or if the reader already knows something about the topic and is familiar with the sort of language it is written in, that's a great help. However, this is not always the case. At school, children often have to read things they don't want to read and often it is not clear to them why they have to be read. In addition, they may start off by knowing nothing at all about the topic and be unfamiliar with that kind of book and the language in it. If children read too slowly then they are likely to have trouble remembering what happened at the beginning of the sentence or paragraph, and so they lose the thread of the meaning.

Of course, teachers are usually aware of these problems and a lot of their teaching is directed towards getting children over them. They encourage children to read a particular book by providing some background knowledge about the topic beforehand (for example, talking about it and showing them photos or pictures). They help children to understand the reasons for reading something, perhaps to find out about the rivers in their neighbourhood, or to follow the instructions for an experiment. Gradually the children are led into using a wider variety of books. You too can help with this. It doesn't matter if you don't know very much about the topic or if you are unfamiliar with the type of books that need to be read. It isn't the content that your child needs help with but rather how to tackle books and get what he or she wants out of them. As adults, we ourselves use a number of different ways of doing this – whether we realise it or not. These include:

- thinking about the subject before we read about it and making a more or less vague guess as to what we shall be reading about
- being clear as to what information we are looking for
- skimming first to get a general idea of content
- all the time being one jump ahead of what we're actually reading, by predicting how a sentence is going to end, what will happen next or what the next bit will be about

We can help our children be more efficient and intelligent readers by encouraging them to do these things.

If your child is having difficulties in understanding here are some things you can do.

- Talk to your child about a topic before he or she starts reading about it, perhaps using the title as a cue. For example, if the title of a text is 'Smuggling Stories', you could ask your child what he or she knows about smuggling, where it occurs, who is likely to do it and why.
- Encourage your child to have a quick look through the book first, noticing pictures, headings and so on, and looking out for words that connect up with what you've just been talking about. This may help to make the connections between a child's background knowledge of the topic and the

particular book which in turn allows your child to start guessing what the stories are going to be about. (The guesses won't be allright of course – there would be no fun if they were – but that's not the point.)

- Your child should be clear about why he or she is going to read a particular book – and you can help with this. All right, it may be that he or she has been told by the teacher to read it, but can you get at the purpose?

- Children often have to answer a set of comprehension questions after reading something. Unfortunately, these are often rather mechanical questions which do not lead to anything more than a rather superficial understanding, but all the same it's useful to be able to cope with them. Tell your child to read the questions first so that he or she knows what to look for when reading. The questions will help your child predict what it is all about in much the same way as illustrations or chapter headings do.

- When reading, children should be encouraged to paraphrase, in their minds what they have just read ('Ah yes, I see, what he really means is so and so', or 'So they've finally escaped') and to guess what is likely to come next. This is something that good readers do all the time. You can help your child learn to do this by getting him or her to stop every now and again at suitable points. 'So what's that bit all about?' or 'What's been happening in the story up to now?' 'What's going to happen next, do you think?' By getting a child to do this for a while you can encourage a child to check up on the meaning of what he or she is reading and predict the next part. In time this will happen automatically. Be careful though that you don't invade his or her privacy and end up by causing irritation.

- Another important way you can improve your child's understanding is to help develop ways of working out the meanings of unfamiliar words. Although I have often suggested that you should encourage your child to keep reading and not worry about the meaning of each word, there may be times when the meaning of a particular word is essential for understanding. Also there are other times when a child is asked to give the meaning of a particular word. Of course, dictionaries come in handy here and I certainly don't mean to discourage their use. However, sometimes a dictionary isn't available and often finding a word in a dictionary and then picking out the right meaning takes up more time than using the context to work out the meaning. Reading the parts (or sentences) both before and after the unfamiliar word often provides useful clues to the meaning. Also it is important to look at the word itself and see if it is similar to other known words. For example, the word 'medicinal', as in 'Use for medicinal purposes only', is likely to have something to do with 'medicine', and the word 'homely', as in 'This homely hotel offers all comforts', is related to the word 'home'.

Extending the range of books

The reading tastes of this age group are very diverse and individual. Fortunately, there is an equally diverse range of books available, which can help to satisfy your child's needs and extend his or her literary experiences. Many of the themes of the books they read when younger, such as everyday life, adventure and fantasy, are still very popular. But now the language and the characterisation are often the things that capture and hold children's attention, though the topic and plot are still important.

An important characteristic of older readers is their need to choose books themselves. Some children still respond well to suggestions made by teachers and parents but many children resist such suggestions. Their selection is mostly based on their friends' and perhaps older brothers' and sisters' advice. Being part of the group has first priority. While we must respect this, it doesn't mean that your child need only read adolescent Mills and Boon type books (if that is the current trend). You can still provide alternatives. Your child may read fashion magazines, hobby magazines, humorous ones, information books, as well as fiction. All of these also count as reading and are in fact sometimes preferred. In this section, however, I only look at fiction books. *The Good Book Guide to Children's Books*, edited by Bing Taylor and Peter Braithwaite, and brought out annually by Penguin, covers the reference and non-fiction book area in detail.

In the list below I have divided a number of fiction books into the categories of fantasy fiction, science fiction, everyday life, humour, adventure, war, picture books and short stories. These categories overlap and are only meant to serve as a general guide. Of course, those listed are just a sprinkling of the many books available. The books chosen will, once again, still be dependent on your child's particular interests, attitude to reading and general knowledge, as well as previous reading experiences. The books cover a very large age range. Some are suitable for the ten to twelve year olds while others are more suitable for the teenage reader. Your child is probably the best judge.

Fiction

Fantasy fiction These books contain stories of other worlds and times. They are highly moral tales involving the eternal struggles of good against evil, with good being triumphant. The hero or heroine usually takes on some task or quest and the effort to fulfil this quest teaches them about life. Some go back into the past and others move from the world as we know it into a fantasy one where the history and geography are quite different from our own.
Tom's Midnight Garden by Philippa Pearce (Puffin)

The Owl Service; Elidor; The Stone Book by Alan Garner (Fontana)
Master of the Grove by Victor Kelleher (Puffin)

Science fiction   These books are also fantasy fiction but here there is a projection into the future and some give a taste of what life might be like on another planet perhaps.
The White Mountains trilogy by John Christopher (Hamish Hamilton/Puffin)
Hitchhiker's Guide to the Galaxy Series by Douglas Adams (Pan)
Out of Time by Aidan Chambers (Bodley Head paperback)
A Wrinkle in Time by Madeline L'Engle (Puffin)

Everyday life   Stories about everyday lives are still extremely popular with this age group. The friendship, school and family stories now include the new conflicts and emotions of adolescence. I believe these stories are extremely useful. They can give children insight into the problems of others, which helps to develop their understanding and tolerance. They can help them face up to and cope with their own problems and they can prepare them for problems that they may encounter later. The best are those that contain characters and events that they can easily identify with and those that stir their emotions (be it sadness or happiness).
The Pigman by Paul Zindel (Puffin)
The One-Eyed Cat by Paula Fox (Puffin)
Displaced Person by Lee Harding (Puffin)

Humour   Children of this age group appreciate stories and language that make them laugh. While many of the books already mentioned, particularly in the everyday life section contain humorous parts, below are some particularly funny books.
Halfway Across the Galaxy and Turn Left (Penguin); *Ratbags and Rascals* by Robin Klein (Dent)
The Secret Diary of Adrian Mole Aged 13$\frac{3}{4}$; The Growing Pains of Adrian Mole by Sue Townsend (Methuen)
Sheep Pig; Queen's Nose by Dick King Smith (Puffin)

Adventure   Older readers love the action, suspense, surprise and setbacks in these exciting tales of survival.
Survival by Russel Evans (Puffin)
My Side of the Mountain; Julie of the Wolves by Jean George (Puffin)
Zed by Rosemary Harris (Magnet)
The Boundary Riders by Joan Phipson (Puffin)
Kept in the Dark by Nina Bawden (Puffin)

War   Stories about children involved in war have a very powerful effect on adolescents. They contain all the ingredients of a good story. They are adventurous, exciting and emotional. The main protagonists are usually children of a similar age and so the readers themselves experience their struggle for survival. These stories are not fantasy stories. The setting provides a description of real events and places which can give children both a picture and an understanding of their own history.

Carrie's War by Nina Bawden (Puffin)
The Silver Sword by Ian Serraillier (Puffin)
I Am David by Anne Holm (Magnet)
The Diary of Anne Frank (Pan)
Little Brother by Allan Baillie (Nelson)

Picture books Many adults are surprised that picture books are suitable for older readers. However, many picture books are enjoyable for both adolescents and their younger brothers and sisters. Such books operate on many different levels. For example, while the five year old can laugh at Willy's antics and appearance in *Willy the Wimp*, the twelve year old can appreciate another level of meaning, that is, Willy's need for acceptance, his lack of self esteem, his efforts to build up his macho strength and the inevitable return to reality. Other picture books have been especially written for this age group. Their artwork is exquisite and it can be appreciated for itself. The art can stir your child's imagination and can also extend the meaning of the written text. The illustrations can capture the interest of the most reluctant reader. Such books also have the advantage that they are short and can be read in one sitting. They encapsulate so many experiences and feelings in such a short space. So much can be discussed and felt.

The Visitors Who Came To Stay by Annalena McAfee (Hamish Hamilton)
The Favershams; *Sir Cedric* by Roy Gerrard (Gollancz)

Short stories Often short stories are appealing because, as with picture books, they can say so much in so few words. The plot, the setting and the characterisation are all compressed into a short space, which can be read in one sitting. They are often ideal for those children who are daunted by the sight and thought of 100 pages to go.

Badger on the Barge and Other Stories by Janni Howker (Julie Macrae / Fontana Lions)
In A Class Of Their Own by Barbara Ireson (Faber)
Feet and Other Stories by Jan Mark (Puffin)

Adult fiction Although there are so many good books specifically written for children, the older ones may well be beginning to enjoy adult literature. Often their interest in a book comes after a television or film dramatisation. Although the translation from book to film is not always successful and in fact often doesn't do justice to the language and characterisation in the original, reading the book of the movie can stimulate interest in an author and help to extend your child's range of reading. It also has the advantage of being a 'popular' thing to do, which is important at this age.

Some books which might come into this category are:
Picnic at Hanging Rock by Joan Lindsay
Rebecca by Daphne du Maurier
The French Lieutenant's Woman by John Fowles

Lord of the Flies by William Golding
Nineteen Eighty-Four by George Orwell
To Kill a Mockingbird by Harper Lee

Non-fiction

The lists that follow contain books which will be helpful for children's school work as well as their particular interests and hobbies. Of course, these are only a sample of the many available. Large bookshops and libraries are likely to have these and many others. As children get older the range of non-fiction books open to them increases, as many books written for adults are suitable for adolescent readers as well. Therefore if your child needs more information than the following books provide, don't hesitate to consult the adult section of both bookshops and libraries.

History

Here are some books about life in previous times, how people lived, what they wore, what their towns looked like:

Peoples of the Past Series (Macdonald Educational) – The Greeks; The Middle Ages; The Vikings; The Celts; The Aztecs; The Normans; The Incas; The Saxons

Fashion Through The Ages Series (Cambridge) – The Clothes They Wore: 17th and 18th Centuries; The Clothes They Wore: 19th and 20th Centuries

The Vikings: Fact and Fiction – Adventures of Young Vikings in Jorvik by Robin Place (Cambridge)

The Romans: Fact and Fiction by Robin Place (Cambridge)

The Seven Wonders of the World by Kenneth McLeish (Cambridge)

The Cambridge Introduction to World History (Cambridge) – The Viking Ships; Life in a Medieval Village; Life in a Medieval Monastery; Building the Medieval Cathedrals; The Growth of a Medieval Town

Our world

Most children have an interest in understanding the geography, the differing landscapes and weather patterns, our natural resources and how these influence the way we live. These books are just a few of the many that give a good introduction to these topics:

The Young Geographer Investigates by Terry Jennings (Oxford) – Deserts; Mountains; Rivers; Tropical Forests; Polar Regions; Temperate Forests, etc.

World Resources Series (Wayland) – Alternative Energy; Dairy Produce; Diamonds; Leather; Nuclear Fuel; Paper; Soya; Textiles

The Living Planet: A Portrait of the Earth by David Attenborough (Collins/ BBC) – based on the excellent TV series

Nature

Past and present animal and plant life interest older readers as well as younger ones. The following books provide details of these that can give children a greater understanding of ecology.

The Seasons Series (Wayland) – Summer; Autumn; Winter; Spring

Body Plans – Animals from the Inside by John Llewellyn-Jones (Cambridge) – paper cut-outs from which children can build up the bodies of animals of different kinds

The Australian Environment Series (Hodder & Stoughton) – Alpine Regions; Coral Reefs; Deserts; Frogs; Insects; Native Plants; Rainforests; Swamps and Estuaries

Nature in Focus Series (Macdonald) – Wildlife in Towns; Life in Ponds and Streams; The Wildlife of Woodlands; Life on the Seashore; The Wildlife of Mountains and Moorlands; The Wildlife of Farmland

Science and technology

Here is a variety of books that can help children investigate and explore the world of science. Some of these provide guidelines for their own investigations, others introduce them to the fast growing world of electronics, others give an understanding of the universe and evolution, while still others provide an in depth look at the human body.

The Young Scientist Investigates Series by Terry Jennings (Oxford) – The Human Body; Pond Life

Exploring Science: Introductory Book by Peter Stanford (Macmillan Australia)

The Amazing Science Amusement Arcade by the Ontario Science Centre (Cambridge University Press)

Scienceworks by the Ontario Science Centre (Angus and Robertson)

The Adventures of Charles Darwin by Peter Ward (Cambridge University Press)

Cambridge Science Universe edited by David Jollands (Cambridge University Press) – Outer Space and Inner Space; Language and Communication; Sight, Light and Colour; Energy, Forces and Resources; Machines, Power and Transport; Measuring and Computing; Earth, Sea and Sky; Patterns of Life on Earth

Cambridge Illustrated Dictionary for Young Scientists edited by David Jollands and Jeanne Stone (Cambridge University Press)

New Technology Series (Rigby Usborne) – Satellites and Space Stations; Solar Power; Robotics; Lasers; Information Revolution

The Human Body; *Facts of Life* by Jonathan Miller and David Pelham (Jonathan Cape)

Computers

As computers become part of our everyday lives, more and more books about them are published. Some are for complete novices, some provide a background to how computers work, some define the many new terms used, some help children do their own programming, while still others provide information on the software that is available. Below are just a few of these:

The Penguin Computing Book by Susan Curran and Ray Curnow (Penguin)

Cambridge Illustrated Dictionary for Young Computer Users by A. Godman and T. Tregear (Cambridge University Press)

A Child's Guide to the Apple Micro; *Amstrad Micro* by John Dewhirst and James Ryan; *Commodore 64*; *BBC Micro*; *Electron Micro* by John Dewhirst; *ZX Spectrum* by John Dewhirst and Rosemary Tennison (Cambridge University Press)

Personal development The changes in the bodies and emotions of adolescent children are examined from a scientific, a personal and a social perspective in the following books:
The Teenage Body Book by Kathy McCoy and Charles Wibblesman (Simon & Schuster)
What's Happening To Me? by Peter Mayle (Sun Books, Melbourne)
Growing Up by S. Meredith (Usborne)

Art There are many books on art. Below are just a few introductory ones:
A World History of Art by Hugh Honour (Macmillan)
Looking At Pictures by Susan Woodford (Cambridge University Press)
The Story of Art by Ernst Gombrich (Phaidon/Penguin)

Culture and civilisation We live in a multicultural society. Our homes, our clothes and the way we live are all influenced by where we live, our personal histories, our beliefs and our customs. By looking at a range of different countries, ways of life and religions, our children are more likely to develop a greater understanding of different cultures, as well as their own background.
City Life Series (Macdonald) – Living in Venice; Living in Hong Kong; Living in Berlin; Living in Sydney; Living in London
My Village Series (Macdonald) – My Village in Nepal; My Village in Morocco; My Village in the Sahara; My Village in India
The Story of the Christians by Jennifer Rye; *The Story of the Jews* by Julia Neuberger; *The Story of Islam* by Antony Kamm; *The Story of the Hindus* by Jacqueline Hirst (Cambridge University Press)
Religions of the World (Wayland) – Christianity; Hinduism; Buddhism; Islam; Judaism; Sikhism

Careers When children begin to think about what they would like to do when they leave school, the following kinds of books which give some insight into the working days of people in a great variety of occupations, are useful:
A Day in the Life Of Series (Wayland) – A Day With an Ambulanceman; A Day With a Fisherman; A Day with a Hairdresser; A Day with a Musician; A Day with a Vet etc.
People at Work (Wayland) – Working at an Airport; Working on a Building Site; Working on a Newspaper; Working for Yourself, etc.
The Armed Forces Series (Wayland) – The Army; The Royal Air Force; The Royal Navy

General There are many non-fiction books that do not fit into the above categories. Some of these listed below are general reference books, while others, like encyclopaedias, cover a very wide range of topics.
Kingfisher Pocket Books (Kingfisher) – Astronomy; Aircraft; Atlas; Dinosaurs; Magic; Wildlife, etc.
Just Look At Series (Macmillan) – Space Exploration; Computers; Prehistoric Life; The Modern Age, etc.

Australian Colour Library Series (Macmillan) – Mammals; Reptiles and Amphibians; Transport; Agriculture; Birds; Plants; Money; Minerals; Australian Explorers
Picture Library Series (Franklin Watts) – Aircraft Carriers; Earthmovers; Farm Machinery; The Moon; Night Sky; Oil Rigs; Space Shuttle; Undersea Machines; Warships, etc.

Activity books The following books are filled with interesting things to make and do. Some are concerned with hobbies, while others contain a variety of different activities.
Beginner's Guides (Rigby Usborne) – Playing Chess; Playing the Guitar; Bicycling and Bike Maintenance; Cameras and Photography; Woodwork; Sewing; My Nature Diary; Our Town
Keep Out of the Kitchen Mum by Jill Cox (André Deutsch)
Usborne's First Cookbook by Angela Wilkes and Stephen Cartwright (Usborne)
Roland Harvey's Incredible Book of Almost Everything by Roland Harvey (Five Mile Press)

Coping with difficulties

In this section I suggest again how parents can help children who can read but don't and children who still can't read.

Children who don't read

As your child moves through upper primary school and secondary school you may find that he or she is reading less. School work is probably more demanding, diversions will have increased and books may no longer be seen as a source of pleasure. Reading may be regarded by your child as something that is part of school and something that keeps him or her away from friends and other leisure activities. Understandably you may be concerned that your child will never take up reading again.

As with children of all ages, we cannot force them to read. With this age group particularly we need to accept that children may want a rest from reading, that their time is already filled with many activities and that they are likely to resist any pressure to read.

So what can you do?

As usual you need a combination of patience and encouragement. Patience, so that you aren't tempted to make reading 'an issue', and encouragement, so that your child still sees that reading matters. Your child still needs to see that reading is worthwhile, still needs to have access to books that interest him or her and still needs to have time to read.

In order to recapture an interest in books your child needs to have fairly long periods of uninterrupted free time. It just doesn't happen between washing up, studying and playing football. Often children will need time out to do nothing but unwind and, like us, collapse in front of the TV for their relaxation. In my own very busy work times I tend to use television more and books less as a source of relaxation. It is only when I have a break from work, such as on holidays, that I am able to find the time needed to 'get into' a book. Many children are the same. Holidays, after exams and convalescence provide the opportunities for children to get back into reading and often the reading habit acquired in these periods sticks.

Letting your child read what he or she wants to read at these times can certainly help. Remember, approval and acceptance from your child's friends is much more important to him or her than your own advice and suggestions. Nevertheless, while you may not be able to choose your child's books you can still provide access to books through making sure that your child is a member of the local library or a book club and by giving book tokens as birthday and Christmas presents.

Books that have been made into movies are suitable for children who don't like to spend a lot of time reading and these often meet with the approval of their friends and classmates. Some examples of good movies and television series based on books are:

The Never Ending Story
Secrets of NIMH (based on the book *Mrs Fisby and the Rats of NIMH* by Robert O'Brien)
Charlotte's Webb
Charlie and the Chocolate Factory
Wind in the Willows

There are also books that have been written after extremely popular movies such as:

Star Wars and *Return of the Jedi*
Wizard of Oz and *Return to Oz*

Meanwhile, try not to be too concerned. Your child may return to reading as school pressures get less. Remember, many adults go through long non-reading periods and return to it later.

Children who can't read

There are a few children at this age who still can't read and certainly it is a cause for concern. It is a very difficult situation and unfortunately there are no miracle cures. It is important that you realise that it isn't up to you to teach your child to read. Your child is likely to reject any attempts you make and even the slightest pressure you place on him or her can result in tension and rebellion. Neither you nor your child need that. Your child will probably be finding it hard enough at school, where he or she will all the time be coming up against the successes of other children.

Nevertheless, it is essential that you don't give up hope. Just as with younger non-readers, your child will still benefit from your support. He or she still needs to believe that they will be able to read. Your child still needs to feel a worthwhile person and that not being able to read doesn't mean not being able to enjoy life.

It is extremely important to talk to your child's teacher. The teacher needs to know of your concerns and your willingness to provide any support needed. Talk to the teacher about the methods he or she is using and ask what you might be able to do at home. Together, with the teacher, you can give your child the idea that reading is desirable and that there is something in it for him or her.

Once again, even at this age it is important that you read to your child. While this may be difficult to start if it isn't already an established habit, it is worthwhile pursuing. By reading to your child you can give him or her the experiences that are available to readers. Just because your child can't read, it doesn't mean he or she can't enjoy stories and benefit from them. Also your child still needs to hear the language and patterns of stories. Apart from the pleasure the language and stories can give, the more familiar your child is with them, the more able he or she will be to be involved with the story and join in. Naturally, the stories you read need to reflect your child's age and interests and not their reading ability. The books shouldn't have oversized letters and look like 'remedial' books, because the stories in such books are unlikely to capture your child's interest. Also they will only confirm their feeling as a failure at reading.

Again, as with all children of this age group, their own choice of books should have priority over what we as adults feel is suitable. There are, however some adolescent non-readers who choose books (often because of their experiences at school) just because they *look* easy rather than because they interest them. They may be looking for readability rather than pleasure in the story. You can help to direct them away from this viewpoint by reading a story that they will enjoy. It can be a story already familiar from television or the movies or perhaps it is about an interest that your child is pursuing. Try to get your child to listen and enjoy the story for the story's sake.

Your child also needs to see that reading is a part of normal life and to believe that he or she is already reading and behaving like a reader. You can encourage reading of labels on food items, signs, ads on television, billboards and titles of movies and films. However, make sure that it doesn't appear like a test, so don't just suddenly ask what does this say or that say. Rather encourage your child to read bits and pieces of things that are part of everyday life. It might be the instructions for a game, or it might simply be finding the time and channel of a new television series. Whatever it is, if your child feels no pressure to perform but understands that reading is providing information, you will be helping him or her become a reader. Remember your child needs confidence and rewards and you, difficult as it may seem, need to have lots of patience and plenty of hope.

Some answers to questions

Does it matter if children only read comics? If so, how can I encourage my child to read 'better' literature?
Not all comic reading is bad. Comics can be amusing and provide light reading for children in the same way as light novels and magazines do for

adults. If comics are only part of a child's reading diet, then they are harmless. However, if comics are your child's only reading matter then certainly it is important to try to encourage a more varied reading diet, as comics, alone, do not help develop good reading habits.

This is so for a number of reasons. First, comics do not contain the real language of stories. The language used is usually conversational and doesn't contain the links and sequencing words that are usually present in written stories. For children to become fluent readers they need to be familiar with not just the spoken form of language but also with the written form, as found in most books. Secondly, children can become dependent on the visual clues provided by the pictures. Whereas pictures are essential to beginner and reluctant readers, it is important that children learn to use other clues to help them understand what they are reading. Thirdly, the stories are often too simple to be interesting and the characters can be so stereotyped that the reader doesn't need to think at all while reading.

If your child becomes used to the language, the pictures, the simple plot and stereotyped characters of comics, he or she may find it difficult to read anything else. To encourage your child to read more widely try asking what he or she likes about comics. If it's the pictures, then suggest some books with pictures, if it's the humour then try funny books, if it's a particular kind of adventure, then pick out some books with similar kinds of adventures. If it's because friends read them, then it is more difficult. You could try providing some better quality comic books, such as the Tintin and Asterix series. There are some writers, such as Raymond Briggs, who use the cartoon strip form excellently as in *When the Wind Blows* (Penguin). There are other books, such as *Chips and Jessie* by Shirley Hughes, that integrate the cartoon form with the narrative. After reading these better quality comics, where the reader needs to be more active, your child may find the ordinary comic boring (but of course he or she may not!).

Does it matter if my child only reads magazines?
Some children enjoy reading magazines because like comics they are generally easy reading. They do not need much concentration as the stories are short, pretty obvious and generally have plenty of pictures. As with comics, magazine reading is all right unless it is the only form of reading. Remember also the influence of friends. Magazine reading may be fine while books can be regarded as a 'no-no'. The experiences that your child shares with friends are probably fed by the information found in the current magazine, whether it is fashion, make-up, cars or computer games.

As with comics, some magazines are better quality than others. Some can extend knowledge in particular areas of interest, so perhaps try steering your child away from light fiction magazines towards those that meet his or her interests and hobby needs.

My child's writing is rather stilted and boring. Is this a reflection of her reading habits?

It might be. Reading and writing are certainly linked in many ways. The books children read provide models for their own writing. The greater the variety of story and language, the more models children have for expressing their own thoughts and ideas. It would be very difficult for a child to write a fairy tale, a science fiction story or a book review without first having read several examples of each. There are also other factors that influence your child's writing. There is more to it than reading models and not all fluent and enthusiastic readers are good writers. Remember that a good story writer is not necessarily good at writing an account of something or a description of how something works. Writers need practice in different types of writing – and children are no different. With luck, your child's teacher will be giving help in this. All the same, it is certainly true that if a child reads a wide variety of different kinds of books it will have a good effect on their language, spoken and written. So a change in what your child is reading can have a positive effect on her writing.

Does it really matter what my child reads as long as she is reading?

Although reading anything is better than not reading at all, a varied and good reading diet is preferable. But what is 'good'? Your child's idea of what is 'good' may be quite different from yours.

I would like to see my own children in their teens read books written by Susan Cooper, Alan Garner, Patricia Wrightson and the like, since I regard these authors' works as 'good literature' because of the way they are written and their content. But I know my children may find other writers just as challenging and more enjoyable. And of course what their friends think of as 'good' is bound to influence them a lot. There is yet another point to consider. Reading 'good' literature prepares children for the tougher demands of what they have to read at school. If children are used to reading only 'junk' material, they may find the other books they need to read too demanding and miss out on all that can be got from them. So try to get them to limber up for reading as they do for sport!

My child reads all the time and has no other interests. Should I discourage her?

Many parents would envy this situation as usually the problem is the reverse. While I can understand that you feel that your child should develop other interests, I wouldn't be too worried and I don't suggest that you try to cut down on reading time. However, if she doesn't have any friends, she may be using books as an escape in order to avoid social contact. If this is so, you may want to think up ways of bringing her more into contact with other children. But if she is happy and well adjusted then don't feel she is missing out on anything. Her world and experiences are certainly expanding all the time.

Are computer games contributing to the current decline in interest in reading?

Certainly computer and video games attract many children and may seem (to adults) to be just another noisy intrusion into our lives. Many of these games, however, are quite constructive and the interaction that goes on between the player and the screen can be stimulating. You will probably find that children get bored with those games that don't ask them to do much. Fortunately computer software for children is improving all the time and many programs go a long way beyond the primitive 'zap! zap!' arcade games that were all the rage. There are problem-solving programs that will hold children's attention and involve them actively for long periods. These may involve reasoning, predicting, maths, language – and still be fun. And there are many kinds of simulation programs that children enjoy, in which they can pretend to be in charge of a ship, searching for treasures etc. – all stimulus to the imagination and, if played in a group, to the use of language. Many programs involve a fair amount of reading and although this calls for a way of reading ('scrolling' over the screen) different from that used in reading a book, it is a useful technique to learn for modern life. Computers, like television, are here to stay and we want our children to learn to use them.

I have very little time but I would still like to encourage my child to read. What can I do?

I know time is often difficult to find. Here are a few things that you can do that don't need much effort or time – but don't expect miracles, as there is really no substitute for spending time on your child's reading.

- Give your child book tokens and subscriptions for magazines for birthday and Christmas presents.
- Suggest your child could team up with friends to go to the library together.
- Suggest your child enters a writing competition. Newspapers, schools and radio programmes often have such competitions. (A recent detective short story competition encouraged quite a large group of teenagers to visit the library and got them really interested in detective stories.)
- Don't criticise what your child is reading, even if you think it isn't quite right.

Chapter Seven

Summing up

I hope this book has convinced you of the important contributions you can make in the development of your child as a reader. Reading is an integral part of life. What we read affects our lives just as the events of our daily lives influence what we get out of reading. Our homes are part of our everyday lives and we cannot ignore the fact that, together with the school, we help our children to learn to read and become and remain, we hope, enthusiastic readers.

We, as parents, can help a lot in this process by reading to our children, praising their successes, working together with the school and giving our children access to many different kinds of books. Of course, this means spending time with our children. In this book I have suggested ways and techniques which I hope will make the time spent both pleasant and fruitful. By making reading a pleasurable activity your child's chances of becoming a keen reader increase and he or she is more likely to benefit from all the joys reading offers.

However, we should also remember that problems do arise and that our children won't always meet our expectations. Our children are individuals. They mature at different rates and their experiences affect them in different ways. We must also recognise that our time is often limited and that our energy is often flagging. Sometimes good intentions can become episodes of frustration and confrontation, both of which we can do without. This book cannot overcome all the problems you will encounter but I hope it has given guidance and support – much the same as you can offer your child.

Books for children

I have divided the following book titles into different age categories. Once again the divisions are guidelines only and many different ages can appreciate those in each category. These lists contain the titles of books mentioned in the suitable materials sections in other chapters, as well as many others.

Two years and under   Ahlberg, Janet and Allen, *The Baby Catalogue; Peepo; Each Peach, Pear Plum* (Kestrel/Puffin)
*Allen, Pamela, *Bertie the Bear; Who Sank the Boat?; Watch Me* (Nelson)
Baum, Louis, *I Want To See The Moon* (Bodley Head)
Bruna, Dick, *B is for Bear; The Little Bird* (Methuen)
Burningham, John, *Little Book Series – The Baby; The Blanket; The Cupboard; The Friend; The Rabbit; The School* (Jonathan Cape)
Campbell, Rod, *Dear Zoo; Oh Dear!; From Gran* (Lothian)

Campbell Pearson, Tracey (Illustrator), *Old MacDonald Had a Farm* (Bodley Head)

*Carle, Eric, *The Very Hungry Caterpillar* (Puffin)

Daly, Niki, *Teddy's Ear; Ben's Gingerbread Man* (Hodder & Stoughton)

Ginsburg, Mirra, *Across the Stream; Good Morning Chick* (Julia Macrae/Puffin)

*Hill, Eric, *Where's Spot?; Spot's First Walk* (Puffin)

*Hughes, Shirley, *Bathwater's Hot; Noisy; When We Went to the Park* (Hodder & Stoughton); *Alfie's Feet; An Evening At Alfie's; Lucy and Tom at the Seaside* (Fontana Lions)

*Hutchins, Pat, *Goodnight Owl; Titch* (Puffin)

Jessel, Camilla, *Baby's Day; Baby's Toys* (Methuen)

Jonas, Anne, *Holes and Peeks* (Julia Macrae)

Kilroy, Sally, *Busy Babies; Babies' Home; Babies' Zoo* (Viking Kestrel)

Maris, Ron, *Are You There Bear?; Is Anyone Home?; My Book* (Julia Macrae)

Ormerod, Jan, *Little One Series: Just like Me; Our Ollie; Young Joe; Silly Goose* (Walker Books)

Oxenbury, Helen, *Animals; Bedtime; Dressing; Family; Friends; Helping; Playing; Working* (Methuen Board Books); *The Birthday Party; The Dancing Class* (Walker Books)

Peppe, Rodney, *Little Numbers; Little Wheels* (Methuen)

Petty, Kate and Kopper, Lisa, *What's That Noise?; Number?; Taste?; Colour?; Smell?; Shape?; Feel?; Size?* (Franklin Watts)

Pienkowski, Jan, *ABC; Colours; Numbers; Home; Shapes; Sizes; Weather* (Heinemann/Puffin)

Rachel, Isadore, *I See; I Hear* (Julia Macrae)

Rey, H.A., *Anybody Home?; Where's My Baby* (Bodley Head)

*Rice, Eve, *Goodnight, Goodnight* (Puffin)

*Tafuri, Nancy, *Rabbit's Morning; Have You Seen My Duckling?* (Julia Macrae)

*Vipont, Elfrida and Briggs, Raymond, *The Elephant and the Bad Baby* (Puffin)

Watanabe, Shigeo, *I'm Going For A Walk; I'm Having A Bath With Papa; I'm Playing With Papa; How Do I Put It On?; I Can Build A House; I Can Do It!* (Bodley Head/Puffin)

Wolde, Gunilla, *Thomas and Emma Series* (Hodder & Stoughton)

*Zachiaris, Thomas and Wanda, *But Where Is The Green Parrot?* (Chatto & Windus)

Three year olds
Alexander, Martha, *Nobody Asked If I Wanted a Baby Sister* (Puffin)

*Allen, Pamela, *Simon Said* (Picture Lions)

Althea *Althea Dinosaur Book*

Argent, Kerry, *Animal Capers* (Omnibus)

*Burningham, John, *Would You Rather; Mr Gumpy's Outing; Mr Gumpy's Motor Car; The Shopping Basket; Time To Get Out Of The Bath, Shirley* (Cape/Puffin)

Caterwill, T. and Argent, K., *Sebastian Lives in a Hat* (Omnibus)

Day, Alexandra, *Good Dog, Carl* (Angus & Robertson)

Dupasquier, Philippe, *Busy Places Series* (Hodder & Stoughton)

*Edwards, Hazel, *There's A Hippopotamus on my Roof Eating Cake* (Hodder & Stoughton)

*Fox, Mem, *Possum Magic* (Omnibus); *Hattie the Fox* (Ashton Scholastic)

Freeman, Don, *Corduroy* (Puffin)

Gag, Wanda, *Millions of Cats* (Puffin)

Garland, Sarah, *Doing the Washing; Going Shopping; Having a Picnic* (Bodley Head)

*Grindley, Sally, *Knock, Knock, Who's There?* (Hamish Hamilton)

*Hall Ets, Marie, *Play With Me; Gilberto and the Wind* (Puffin)

Hewett, Anita, *Mrs Mopple's Washing Line* (Puffin)

Howell, Lynne and Richard, *Winifred's New Bed* (Hamish Hamilton)

*Hughes, Shirley, *Alfie Gets In First; Alfie Gives A Hand; Dogger; Moving Mollie; Sally's Secret* (Picture Lions)*; Up and Up* (Puffin)

*Hutchins, Pat, *Rosie's Walk; Don't Forget the Bacon; You'll Soon Grow Into Them Titch; Happy Birthday Sam; The Wind Blew; One Hunter* (Puffin)

Keller, Holly, *Henry's Picnic* (Julia Macrae)

Kerr, Judith, *The Tiger Who Came To Tea* (Lions)

Ormerod, Jan, *Sunshine; Moonlight* (Puffin)

Pomerantz and Barton, B., *Where's the Bear* (Julia Macrae)

*Rice, Eve, *Benny Bakes a Cake; New Blue Shoes* (Puffin)

*Sutton, Eve, *My Cat Likes to Hide in Boxes* (Puffin)

Wagner, Jenny, *Aranea – A Story About a Spider* (Puffin)

*Wells, Rosemary, *Noisy Nora; Timothy Goes To School* (Puffin)

Wild, Margaret, *There's A Sea in My Bedroom* (Nelson)

Wildsmith, Brian, *The Trunk; Cat on the Mat; Whose Shoes; All Fall Down; The Nest; The Island; The Apple Bird; Toot Toot; Give a Dog a Bone* (Oxford)

Zion, Gene, *Harry the Dirty Dog; Harry By The Sea* (Puffin)

Four year olds
*Allen, Pamela, *Lion in the Night* (Nelson)*; Mr Archimede's Bath* (Picture Lions)

Anno, *Anno's Counting Book* (Bodley Head)

*Ardizzone, Edward, *Little Tim and the Brave Sea Captain; Tim to the Rescue* (Puffin)

*Armitage, Ronda and David, *A Lighthouse Keeper's Lunch; The Lighthouse Keeper's Catastrophe; Icecreams for Rosie* (André Deutsch/Puffin)

*Blake, Quentin, *Mister Magnolia* (Fontana Lions)

Brichta, Alex, *Wishwhat* (Oxford)

Brown, Ruth, *A Dark, Dark Tale* (Hippo)*; The Big Sneeze; My Cat Flossie* (Andersen)

Browne, Anthony, *Willy the Wimp; Willy the Champ* (Julia Macrae/Puffin)*; Gorilla* (Magnet)*; A Walk in the Park; Through the Magic Mirror* (Hamish Hamilton)

*Carle, Eric, *The Mixed-up Chameleon; The Bad-tempered Ladybird* (Puffin)*; The Very Busy Spider* (Hamish Hamilton)

Dahl, Roald, *The Enormous Crocodile* (Puffin)

Denton, Terry, *Felix and Alexander* (Oxford)

Hedderwick, Mairi, *Katie Morag Delivers the Mail; Katie Morag and the Two Grandmothers; Katie Morag and the Tiresome Ted* (Hyland House)

*Hutchins, Pat, *The Very Worst Monster* (Bodley Head)*; Changes, Changes; The Surprise Party* (Puffin)

Lester, Alison, *Clive Eats Aligators* (Oxford)

Morag, Loh, *The Kinder Hat* (Hyland House)

*Nicoll, Helen, *Meg and Mog; Meg's Eggs; Meg on the Moon* (Puffin)

*Oram, Hiawyn and Kitamura, Satoshi, *Angry Arthur; In the Attic; Ned and the Joyabaloo* (Andersen/Puffin)

*Ormerod, Jan, *Chicken Licken* (Hodder & Stoughton)

*Park, Ruth and Niland, Ruth, *When the Wind Changed* (Picture Lions)

*Prater, John, *You Can't Catch Me* (Bodley Head)
Ryan, John, *Captain Pugwash* (Puffin)
*Sendak, Maurice, *Where the Wild Things Are* (Puffin)
*Stevenson, James, *What's Under My Bed?* (Victor Gollancz)
Stinson, Kathy, *Red is Best* (Oxford)
Sumiko, *My School* (Heinemann)
*Vincent, Gabrielle, *Ernest and Celestine; Merry Christmas, Ernest and Celestine; Bravo Ernest and Celestine* (Puffin)
*Wagner, Jenny, *John Brown, Rose and the Midnight Cat* (Puffin)
*Wells, Rosemary, *Benjamin and Tulip* (Puffin)
*Willis, Jeanne, *The Tale of Mucky Mabel* (Andersen)
Willis, Jeanne and Varley, Susan, *The Monster Bed* (Andersen)

Nursery rhymes

Briggs, Raymond, *The Mother Goose Treasury* (Puffin)
Lines, Kathleen and Jones, Harold, *Lavender's Blue* (Oxford)
Matterson, Elizabeth, *This Little Puffin* (Puffin)
Opie, Iona and Peter, *The Oxford Nursery Rhyme Book* (Oxford)
Ormerod, Jan, *Rhymes Around The Day* (Puffin)
Voake, Charlotte, *Over the Moon* (Hodder & Stoughton)

Poetry for pre-school children

Butler, Dorothy, *For Me, Me, Me; Poems for the Very Young* (Hodder & Stoughton)
Foster, John, *A Very First Poetry Book* (Oxford)
Rosen, Michael and Blake, Quentin, *Don't Put Mustard in the Custard* (André Deutsch)
Scott-Mitchell, Clare, *When a Goose Meets a Moose* (Methuen)

Five to six year olds
Picture books

See also those marked with an asterisk * in the previous lists.
Anno, *Anno's Journey* (Bodley Head)
Aliki, *Feelings* (Bodley Head)
Allen, Pamela, *Herbert and Harry* (Nelson)
Ardizzone, E. and A., *The Little Girl and the Tiny Doll* (Puffin)
Bang, Molly, *The Paper Crane* (Julia Macrae)
Blume, Judy, *The Pain and the Great One* (Heinemann)
Briggs, Raymond, *Jim and the Beanstalk* (Hamish Hamilton)
Browne, Anthony, *The Piggy Book* (Julia Macrae)
Cole, Babette, *The Trouble With Mum; The Trouble With Dad* (Puffin); *The Slimy Book* (Jonathan Cape)
De Brunhoff, Jean and Laurent, *Babar and the Little Elephant Series* (Methuen)
Dematons, Charlotte, *The Elephant from the Skip* (Bodley Head)
Flournoy, Valerie, *The Patchwork Quilt* (Bodley Head)
Frizzel, Judy and Dick, *Sam and the Dog from the Sea* (Heinemann)
Gray, Nigel, *I'll Take You to Mrs Cole* (Andersen)
Griffith, Helen, *Nata* (Julia Macrae)
Hoban, Russell, *A Baby Sister for Frances; A Birthday for Frances; Bedtime for Frances; Bread and Jam for Frances* (Puffin)
Hutchins, Pat, *Clocks and More Clocks* (Puffin); *The Doorbell Rang* (Bodley Head)
Kent, J., *The Fat Cat* (Puffin)
Krasilovsky, Phyliss, *The Cow Who Fell in the Canal* (Puffin)
Martin, Rodney, *There's a Dinosaur in the Park* (Keystone Picture Books)

Milne, A.A., *Winnie the Pooh; The House at Pooh Corner* (Methuen)
Morimoto, Junko, *The Inch Boy* (Collins)
Parish, P., *Amelia Bedelia* (World's Work)
Roennfeldt, Robert, *Tiddalick, The Frog Who Caused the Flood* (Puffin)
Rose, Gerald, *The Bag of Wind; The Bird Garden* (Bodley Head)
Ross, Tony, *I'm Coming to Get You* (Andersen)
Sendak, Maurice, *The Sign on Rosie's Door; In the Night Kitchen* (Bodley Head)
Stevenson, James, *Could Be Worse* (Viking Kestrel)
Viorst, Judith, *Alexander and the Terrible, Horrible, No Good, Very Bad Day* (Angus & Robertson)
Vivas, Julie, *The Nativity* (Omnibus)
Waddell, Martin, *Going West* (Andersen/Puffin)
Williams, Vera B., *A Chair for my Mother; Something Special for Me* (Julia Macrae)
Zolotow, Charlotte, *Mr Rabbit and the Lovely Present* (Bodley Head)

Story books Ahlberg, Allan, *Happy Family Series* (Puffin)
Corrin, Sara and Stephen, *Stories for Five Year Olds; Stories for Six Year Olds* (Faber/Puffin)
Hutchins, Pat, *King Henry's Palace; The Tale of Thomas Mead; The Train Set* (Bodley Head)
Lobel, Arnold, *Frog and Toad Series* (Puffin)
Mahy, Margaret, *A Lion in the Meadow and Other Stories* (Dent/Puffin)
Oldfield, Pamela, *Helter Skelter: Stories for Six Year Olds* (Blackie/Knight)
Pearce, Philippa, *Lion at School and Other Stories* (Viking Kestrel)
Proysen, Alf, *Mr Pepperpot Series* (Puffin)

Cartwheels published by Hamish Hamilton: Allen, Linda, *Meeko and Mirrabel;* Ball, Brian, *Look Out, Duggy Dog;* Lavelle, Sheila, *Harry's Aunt;* Lavelle, Lambert, *The Half-Term Rabbit;* Sefton, Catherine, *The Ghost Ship*

Read Along Stories published by Cambridge University Press

Folk and fairy tales Alderson, Brian, *The Brothers Grimm: Popular Folk Tales* (Viking Kestrel)
Ardizzone, Edward, *Ardizzone's Hans Andersen – 14 Classic Tales* (André Deutsch)
Baker, Margaret, *Tell Them Again Tales* (Hodder & Stoughton)
Berg, Leila, *Topsy Turvy Tales* (Methuen)
Chapman, Jean, *Tell Me A Tale; Tell Me Another Tale* (Hodder & Stoughton)
Cresswell, Helen, *At The Stroke of Midnight* (Collins)
Fadiman, Clifton, *The Puffin Children's Treasury* (Puffin)
Gag, Wanda, *Tales from Grimm* (Faber)
Ireson, Barbara, *The Faber Book of Nursery Stories* (Faber)
Jones, Terry, *Fairy Tales* (Puffin)
Haviland, Virginia (editor), *The Fairy Tale Treasury* (Hamish Hamilton/Puffin)
Lewis, Naomi, *Hans Christian Andersen: The Snow Queen* (Puffin)
Montogomery, Norah, *To Read and To Tell* (Bodley Head)
Oxenbury, Helen, *The Helen Oxenbury Nursery Story Book* (Heinemann)
Wildsmith, Brian, *La Fontaine, Fables: The Lion and the Rat; The North Wind and the Sun* (Oxford)

Poetry   Bennett, Jill, *Helen Oxenbury's Tiny Tim* (Picture Lions)
Butler, Dorothy, *I Will Build You A House* (Hodder & Stoughton)
Corrin, Sara and Stephen, *Once Upon a Rhyme: 101 Poems for Young Children* (Faber/Puffin)
Foreman, Michael, *A Child's Garden of Verse* (Gollancz)
Foster, John, *A First Poetry Book* (Oxford)
Ireson, Barbara, *The Young Puffin Book of Verse* (Puffin)
Milne, A.A., *Christopher Robin's Verse Book* (Methuen)
Nicoll, Helen (editor), *Poems for Seven Year Olds and Under* (Viking Kestrel/Puffin)
Untermayer, Louis, *The Golden Treasury of Poetry* (Collins)

Seven to nine year olds
Picture books   Anno, *Anno's Flea Market* (Bodley Head)
Beni, Ruth, *Sir Baldergog the Great* (André Deutsch)
Blake, Quentin, *The Story of the Dancing Frog* (Jonathan Cape)
Bolton, Barbara, *Edward Wilkins and His Friend Gwendaline* (Angus & Robertson)
Crabtree, Judith, *The Sparrow's Story at the King's Command* (Oxford)
Dahl, Roald, *The Giraffe, The Pelly and Me* (Bodley Head)
Dupasquier, Philippe, *Dear Daddy* (André Deutsch)
Edwards, Tony, *Ralph the Rhino* (Wellington Lane Press)
Fox, Mem, *Wilfred Partridge Gordon MacDonald* (Omnibus)
Hathorne, Libby, *The Tram to Bondi Beach* (Methuen)
Klein, Robin, *The Princess Who Hated It* (Omnibus)
Lobel, Arnold, *Ming Lo Moves the Mountain* (Julia Macrae)
Mattingley, Christobel, *Rummage* (Angus & Robertson)
McAfee, Analena, *The Visitors Who Came To Stay* (Hamish Hamilton)
Ungerer, Tom, *The Beast of Monsieur Racine* (Bodley Head)

Story books with pictures   Brown, Jeff, *Flat Stanley* (Methuen/Magnet)
Dahl, Roald, *The Magic Finger; The Twits; Fantastic Mr Fox* (Puffin)
Dann, Max, *Bernice Knows Best; One Night at Lottie's Place* (Oxford)
Dumas, Philippe, *Laura and the Bandits* (Lions)
Hoban, Russell, *Dinner at Alberta's* (Puffin)
Hughes, Shirley, *It's Too Frightening For Me* (Puffin); *Chips and Jessie; Another Helping for Chips* (Bodley Head)
Klein, Robin, *Thing; Thingnapped* (Oxford)
Mahy, Margaret, *The Witch in the Cherry Tree; Leaf Magic* (Dent)
Pary Heide, Florence, *The Shrinking of Treehorn; Treehorn's Treasure* (Puffin)
Sendak, Maurice, *Higglety Pigglety Pop! or There Must Be More to Life* (Bodley Head)

Banana Books published by Heinemann: Blume, Judy, *Freckle Juice;* Crossley-Holland, Kevin, *Storm;* Darke, Marjorie, *Imp;* Fine, Anne, *Scaredy-Cat;* Hill, Douglas, *The Moon Monsters; How Jennifer (and Speckle) Saved the Earth;* Hoffman, Mary, *Beware, Princess!;* Impey, Rose, *Who's A Clever Girl, Then?;* King Smith, Dick, *Lightning Fred; Yob;* Lavelle, Sheila, *The Big Stink; The Disappearing Granny;* Lively, Penelope, *Dragon Trouble;* Older, Jules, *Jane and the Pirates;* Pilling, Anne, *No Guns, No Oranges;* Powling, Chris, *The Phantom Carwash;* Tennant, Jane, *The Ghost Child;* Ure, Jennifer, *Brenda the Bold*

Blackbird Books published by Julia Macrae: Ashley, Bernard, *Dinner Ladies Don't Count;* Bond, Ruskin, *Earthquake; Flames in the Forest; Getting Granny's Glasses; Tigers Forever;* Gardam, Jane, *Bridget and William;* Hendry, Diana, *Fiona Finds Her Tongue;* Smith, Joan, *Grandmother's Donkey;* Stinton, Judith, *The Apple-Tree Man;* Williamson, Roger, *Romany Rat; The Cheesemaker and the Giant*

Gazelle Books published by Hamish Hamilton: Allen, Joy, *Boots for Charlie; Cup Final for Charlie; Goal for Charlie; Stick to It Charlie;* Hughson, Anne, *Ragbag;* Newman, Majorie, *Burnt Sausages and Custard;* Ruffell, Anne, *Too Small*

Toppers published by André Deutsch: Alcock, Vivien, *Wait and See;* Cresswell, Helen, *Greedy Alice;* Hoffman, Mary, *The Second-Hand Ghost;* King-Smith, Dick, *E.S.P.;* Lavelle, Sheila, *The Chocolate Candy Kid;* Prince, Alison, *A Job for Merv*

Story books   Adler, D., *The 4th Floor Twins and the Fish Snitch Mystery; The 4th Floor Twins and the Fortune Cookie Chase* (Viking Kestrel/Penguin)
Ahlberg, Janet and Allen, *Jeremiah and the Dark Woods* (Kestrel/Lions)
Aiken, Joan, *A Necklace of Raindrops; Tales of a One-Way Street* (Puffin); *The Last Slice of a Rainbow and Other Short Stories* (Jonathan Cape)
Arkle, Phyllis, *The Village Dinosaur; The Railway Cat* (Puffin)
Ashley, Bernard, *Bicycles Don't Fly; Flying Backwards* (Puffin)
Ball, Duncan, *Selby's Secret* (Angus & Robertson)
Blume, Judy, *Superfudge; Tales of a 4th Grade Nothing* (Piccolo)
Brisley, Joyce, *Milly Molly Mandy Series* (Puffin)
Carpenter, Humphrey, *Mr Majeika* (Puffin)
Cleary, Beverly, *Ramona Series; Ralph S. Mouse; The Mouse and the Motorcycle; Runaway Ralph* (Puffin)
Cook, Patrick, *Elmer the Rat* (Puffin)
Dahl, Roald, *George's Marvellous Medicine; Charlie and the Chocolate Factory; James and The Giant Peach; The Witches; The BFG* (Puffin)
Dann, Max, *Going Bananas; Ernest Pickle's Remarkable Robot; Adventures of My Worst Best Friend* (Oxford)
Edwards, Dorothy, *My Naughty Little Sister Series* (Methuen/Magnet)
Greenwood, Ted, *Marley and His Friends* (Puffin)
Hathorn, Libby, *Paola's Secret* (Methuen)
Hughes, Shirley, *Here Comes Charlie Moon; Charlie Moon and the Big Bonanza Bust Up* (Lions)
Hunter, Norman, *The Incredible Adventures of Professor Branestawm* (Puffin)
Hutchins, Pat, *Follow That Bus; The House That Sailed Away; The Curse of the Egyptian Mummy; The Mona Lisa Mystery* (Lions)
Joy, Margaret, *Tales from Allotment Lane School* (Puffin)
Klein, Robin, *Junk Castle; Penny Pollard's Diary; Penny Pollard's Letters* (Oxford)
Lavelle, Sheila, *My Best Fiend Series* (Hamish Hamilton/Lions)
Lewis, C.S., *The Lion, The Witch and the Wardrobe* (Collins/Puffin)
Lindgreen, Astrid, *Pippi Longstocking Series* (Puffin)
Lurie, Morris, *Toby's Millions*
Mahy, Margaret, *The Great Piratical Rumbustification* (Puffin)
Mark, Jan, *The Dead Letter Box* (Puffin)

Mattingley, Christobel, *Duck Boy* (Puffin)
McCall Smith, Alexander, *The Perfect Hamburger* (Puffin)
Morgan, Helen, *Meet Mary Kate Series* (Puffin)
Murphy, Jill, *The Worst Witch Series* (Puffin)
Nash, Margaret, *Rat Saturday* (Puffin)
Norton, Mary, *The Borrowers Series* (Puffin)
Nostlinger, Christina, *Lollipop; Conrad; Mr Bat's Great New Invention* (Andersen)
Park, Ruth, *Callie's Castle* (Angus & Robertson)
Phipson, Joan, *Hide Till Daytime* (Puffin)
Rodda, Emily, *Something Special* (Puffin)
Storr, Catherine, *Lucy; Lucy Runs Away; Tales of Clever Polly and the Stupid Wolf* (Puffin)
Stuart Barry, Margaret, *The Witch of Monopoly Manor* (Lions)
Tomlinson, Jill, *The Owl Who Was Afraid of the Dark* (Puffin)
Townsend, Hazel, *The Vanishing Gran; The Siege of Cobb Street School; Danny Don't Jump; The Great Icecream Crime; The Speckled Panic; The Choking Peril* (Andersen)
Wagner, Jenny, *The Nimbin* (Puffin)
White, E.B., *Charlotte's Webb* (Puffin)
White, Osmar, *The Superoo of Mungaloo; McGurk and the Lost Atoll; The Further Adventures of Dr A.A.A. McGurk, M.D.* (Puffin)
Yeoman, John, *The Hermit and the Bear* (Puffin); *The Boy Who Sprouted Antlers* (Lions)
Zabel, Jennifer, *Mr Berry's Icecream Parlour* (Puffin)

Poetry   Ahlberg, Allen, *Please Mrs Butler* (Puffin)
Dahl, Roald, *Revolting Rhymes; Dirty Beasts;* (Puffin)
Factor, June, *Far Out Brussel Sprout; All Right Vegemite; A First Australian Poetry Book* (Oxford)
Fatchen, Max, *Wry Rhymes for Troublesome Times* (Oxford)
Fisher, Robert, *Amazing Monsters – Verses to Thrill and Chill* (Faber)
Heylen & Jellet, *Someone's Flying Balloons* (Omnibus/Cambridge)
Klein, Robin, *Snakes and Ladders* (Dent)
Lobel, Arnold, *Whiskers and Rhymes* (Julia Macrae)
McLeod, Doug, *In the Garden of Bad Things* (Puffin)
Milligan, Spike, *Unspun Socks from a Chicken's Laundry; Silly Verse for Kids* (Puffin)
Scott-Mitchell, Clare, *Apples from Hurricane Street* (Methuen)
Silverstein, Shel, *A Light In The Attic; Where the Sidewalk Ends* (Jonathan Cape)
Wright, Kit, *Poems for Nine Year Olds and Under* (Kestrel)

Ten to twelve years   Aiken, Joan, *Mortimer Says Nothing* (Jonathan Cape)
Anno, *Hat Tricks; Multiplying Jar; Anno's Three Little Pigs* (Bodley Head)
Ashley, Bernard, *Break in the Sun* (Puffin)
Baille, Allan, *Adrift; Riverman; Little Brother* (Nelson)
Bawden, Nina, *Rebel on the Rock; Carrie's War; A Handful of Thieves; On the Run; The Peppermint Pig; The Witches' Daughter; Kept in the Dark* (Puffin)
Byers, Betsy, *The Pinballs; The Eighteenth Emergency; The Last Slice of Rainbow* (Bodley Head/Puffin); *The Computer Nut* (Bodley Head); *The Midnight Fox; The TV Kid; The Cartoonist; The House of Wings* (Puffin)

Carr, Robert Vaughan, *Firestorm* (Nelson)

Chambers, Aidan, *Seal Secret; The Present Takers; Out of Time* (Bodley Head); *Ghost After Ghost* (Kestrel)

Cleary, Beverly, *Dear Mr Henshaw* (Puffin)

Cooper, Susan, *The Dark is Rising Series* (Puffin)

Cross, Gillian, *The Demon Headmaster* (Puffin)

Dahl, Roald, *The Boy* (Jonathan Cape/Puffin); *Going Solo* (Jonathan Cape)

De St-Exupéry, Antoine, *The Little Prince* (Piccolo)

Dejong, Meindert, *The House of 60 Fathers* (Puffin)

Fatchen, Max, *Chase Through the Night* (Magnet)

Fisk, Nicholas, *Bonkers Clocks* (Viking Kestrel); *Grinny; You Remember Me!* (Puffin)

Flanagan, Joan, *The Dingbat Spies* (Puffin)

Fowler, Thurley, *The Green Wind* (Rigby)

French, Simon, *Cannily, Cannily* (Puffin)

Garfield, Leon, *Jack Holborn; Mr Corbett's Ghost; Smith* (Puffin)

Garner, Alan, *The Stone Book* (Fontana)

Gee, Maurice, *The Halfmen of O* (Puffin); *The Priests of Ferris* (Oxford)

Goscinny and Uderzo, *Asterix Series* (Knight); *Tin Tin* (Magnet)

Hadley, Eric and Tessa, *Legends of Earth, Air, Fire and Water; Legends of the Sun and Moon* (Cambridge)

Hoban, Russell, *The Dancing Tigers* (Cape)

Horowitz, Anthony, *Kingfisher Book of Myths and Legends* (Kingfisher)

Kavanagh, Michael, *Telling Tales; A Swag of Stories* (Oxford)

Kaye, M.M., *The Ordinary Princess* (Puffin)

Kemp, Gene, *Jason Bodger and the Priory Ghost* (Faber); *The Turbulent Term of Tyke Tiler* (Puffin)

Kerven, Rosalind, *Legends of the Animal World* (Cambridge)

King Smith, Dick, *The Sheep Pig; The Queen's Nose; Harry's Mad* (Gollancz/ Puffin)

Klein, Robin, *The Boss of the Pool; The Enemies* (Angus & Robertson); *Hating Alison Ashley* (Puffin); *Ratbags and Rascals* (Dent); *Halfway Across the Galaxy and Turn Left; Games* (Viking/Kestrel)

Lively, Penelope, *The Ghost of Thomas Kemp; Astercote* (Puffin)

Lunn, Janet, *The Root Cellar* (Puffin)

MacDonald, Caroline, *Visitors* (Nelson)

McCutcheon, Elsie, *The Summer of the Zepellin* (Puffin); *The Rat War* (Dent)

McKinley, Robin, *The Door in the Hedge* (Julia Macrae)

Mahy, Margaret, *The Chewing-Gum Rescue and Other Stories; The Birthday Burglar and a Very Wicked Headmistress; The Haunting; The Library and the Robbers; The Pirates' Mixed-up Voyage* (Dent); *The Great Practical Rumbustification; Raging Robots and Unruly Robots* (Puffin)

Majorian, Michelle, *Goodnight Mr Tom* (Puffin)

Mark, Jan, *Handles; Nothing to be Afraid Of; Thunder and Lightnings* (Puffin); *Hairs in the Palm of the Hand* (Kestrel)

Mebs, Gundrum, *Sunday's Child* (Andersen)

Nesbit, E., *The Railway Children; The Enchanted Castle* (Puffin)

Neville, Emily, *It's Like This Cat* (Puffin)

Nostlinger, Christine, *The Cucumber King* (Beaver Books)

O'Brien, Robert C., *Mrs Frisby and the Rats of NIMH* (Puffin)

Pearce, Philippa, *Tom's Midnight Garden; A Dog So Small* (Puffin)

Peyton, K.M., *Who Sir, Me Sir* (Puffin)

Pilling, Anne, *The Year of the Worm* (Faber)

Reid Banks, Lynne, *I, Houdini; The Indian in the Cupboard; The Fairy Rebel* (Dent)

Rodgers, Mary, *Freaky Friday* (Puffin)

Sendak, Maurice, *Higglety Pigglety Pop! Or There Must Be More To Life* (Bodley Head)

Stow, Randolf, *Midnite* (Puffin)

Ure, Jean, *Hi There Supermouse!* (Puffin)

Van Allsburg, Chris, *Mysteries of Harris Burdick; The Wreck of the Zephyr* (Andersen)

Vautier, Ghislaine, adapted by McLeish, Kenneth, *The Way of the Stars; The Shining Stars* (Cambridge)

Waters, Fiona, *The Cat King's Daughter and Other Stories* (Magnet)

Wheatley, Nadia, *Five Times Dizzy; Dancing in the Anzac Deli* (Oxford)

White, E.B., *Charlotte's Web* (Hamish Hamilton/Puffin)

Wrightson, Patricia, *I Own the Racehorse!* (Puffin)

Thirteen plus
Short stories

Chambers, Aidan, *A Sporting Chance* (Bodley Head)

Dahl, Roald, *The Wonderful Story of Henry Sugar and Six More* (Puffin)

Gregory, Susan, *Martini-In-The-Rock* (Puffin)

Howker, Janni, *Badger on the Barge and Other Stories* (Julia Macrae)

Ireson, Barbara, *In a Class of Their Own* (Faber)

Kavanagh, Michael, *A Bundle of Yarns* (Oxford)

Mark, Jan, *Feet and Other Stories* (Puffin Plus)

Westall, Robert, *The Haunting of Chas McGill and Other Stories* (Puffin)

Woodford, Peggy, *Misfits* (Bodley Head)

Novels

Adams, Douglas, *Hitchhiker's Guide to the Galaxy Series* (Pan)

Adams, Richard, *Watership Down* (Penguin)

Aldridge, James, *The True Story of Lilly Stubeck* (Hyland House)

Ashley, Bernard, *Break in the Sun; High Pavement Blues* (Puffin)

Atterton, Julian, *The Fire of the Kings* (Julia Macrae)

Babbit, Natalie, *Goody Hall; Herbert Rowbarge* (Dent)

Barnett, Gillian, *The Inside Hedge Story* (Oxford)

Blume, Judy, *Tiger Eyes* (Piccolo)

Briggs, Raymond, *When the Wind Blows* (Penguin)

Byers, Betsy, *Cracker Jackson* (Bodley Head)

Chambers, Aidan, *Breaktime; Dance on My Grave* (Bodley Head)

Christopher, John, *The White Mountains* (Puffin)

Cleary, Beverly, *Fifteen; Dear Mr Henshaw* (Puffin)

Cooper, Susan, *Seaward* (Puffin)

Cormier, Robert, *I Am The Cheese; The Chocolate War* (Fontana Lions)

Dickinson, Peter, *The Blue Hawk* (Puffin)

Evans, Russel, *Survival* (Puffin)

Francis, Helen, *Edge of Fear* (Omnibus/Puffin)

Forest, Antonia, *Autumn Term; End of Term; The Attic Term; The Cricket Term* (Puffin)

Fox, Paula, *The One-Eyed Cat* (Puffin)

Frank, Anne, *The Diary of Anne Frank* (Pan)

Gardam, Jane, *The Summer After The Funeral* (Puffin)

Garfield, Leon, *John Diamond* (Puffin)

Garner, Alan, *Red Shift; The Owl Service* (Collin/Lions)*; Elidor* (Fontana)

George, Jean, *My Side of the Mountain; Julie of the Wolves* (Puffin)

Gleeson, Libby, *Eleanor, Elizabeth* (Angus & Robertson/Puffin)

Godden, Rumer, *The Greengaye Summer* (Puffin)

Green, Bette, *Summer of my German soldier* (Puffin)

Harding, Lee, *Displaced Person* (Puffin)

Harris, Rosemary, *Zed* (Magnet)

Hautzig, Esther, *The Endless Steppe* (Puffin)

Heinlein, Robert A., *Citizen of the Galaxy* (Puffin)

Herbert, Fred, *Dune* (New English Library)

Hinton, S.E., *The Outsiders* (Fontana Lions)

Holm, Anne, *I Am David* (Magnet)

Hughes, Monica, *Devil on My Back; Hunter in the Dark; The Sandwriter* (Julia Macrae)*; Crisis on Conshelf; The Keeper of Isis Light Series; Space Trap; Ring-Rise, Ring Set* (Magnet)

Hughes, Ted, *Iron Man* (Faber)

Hunt, Peter, *A Step Off the Path* (Julia Macrae)

Innocenti, Roberto, *Rose Blanche* (Bodley Head)

Kaye, Geraldine, *Comfort Herself* (André Deutsch)

Keeping, Charles, *Sammy Streetsinger; The Highwayman; The Lady of Shalott* (Oxford)

Kelleher, Victor, *Master of the Grove; Papio* (Puffin)

Kemp, Gene, *Gowie Corby Plays Chicken; No Place Like; Charlie Lewis Plays For Time* (Puffin)

Kerr, Judith, *When Hitler Stole the Pink Rabbit* (Fontana/Lions)

Klein, Robin, *People Might Hear You* (Puffin)

Lawrence, Louise, *Children of the Dust* (Bodley Head)

L'Engle, Madeleine, *A Wrinkle in Time* (Puffin)

Le Guin, Ursula, *Wizard of Earthsea; The Tombs of Atuan; The Farthest Shore* (Puffin)

Lingard, Joan, *The File on Fraulein Berg* (Julia Macrae)

Little, Jean, *Mama's Going to Buy You a Mockingbird* (Puffin)

MacIntyre, Elizabeth, *A Wonderful Way to Learn the Language* (Hodder & Stoughton)

McKinley, Robin, *Beauty; The Door in the Hedge; The Hero and the Crown* (Julia Macrae)

Mahy, Margaret, *The Catalogue of the Universe; The Changeover; The Tricksters* (Dent)*; The Haunting* (Fontana)

Mark, Jan, *Trouble Half-Way* (Viking Kestrel)*; The Ennead; Hairs in the Palm of My Hand; Handles* (Puffin)

Needle, Jane, *A Game of Soldiers* (Fontana Lions)

Neville, Emily, *It's Like This Cat* (Puffin)

Orlev, Uri, *The Island on Bird St* (Hutchinson)

Park, Ruth, *Playing Beatie Bow* (Puffin)*; My Sister Sib* (Viking Kestrel)

Paterson, Katherine, *Bridge to Terabithia; Jacob Have I Loved* (Puffin)

Paton Walsh, Jill, *A Parcel of Patterns* (Puffin)

Pearce, Philippa, *Minnow on the Say* (Puffin)

Peyton, K.M., *The Flambards* (Puffin)

Phipson, Joan, *The Boundary Riders* (Puffin)

Reid Banks, Lynne, *One More River* (Puffin)*; My Darling Villain; The Writing on the Wall* (Bodley Head)

Reiss, Johanna, *The Upstairs Room* (Puffin)

Scott, Bill, *Darkness Under the Hills* (Oxford)

Serrailier, Ian, *The Silver Sword* (Puffin)

Shapcott, Thomas, *Holiday of the Icon* (Puffin)

Speare, Elizabeth, *The Sign of the Beaver; The Witch of Blackbird Pond* (Puffin)

Stoddat, Eleanor, *When the Mountains Change Their Tune* (Methuen)

Stranger, Joyce, *The Hound of Darkness* (Dent)

Tolkien, J.R.R., *The Hobbit; The Lord of the Rings* (Unwin Paperbacks)

Townsend, John Rowe, *Cloudy Bright* (Puffin)

Townsend, Sue, *The Secret Diary of Adrian Mole aged 13¾; The Growing Pains of Adrian Mole* (Methuen)

Ure, Jean, *A Proper Little Nooryelf; If It Weren't for Sebastian* (Puffin)

Voight, Cynthia, *Homecoming* (Collins)*; A Solitary Blue* (Atheneum)*; Dicey's Song* (Fontana Lions)

Wesley, Mary, *The 6th Seal* (Dent)

Westall, Robert, *Fathom Five; The Machine-Gunners* (Puffin)

Wrightson, Patricia, *An Older Kind of Magic; The Wirrun Trilogy; A Little Fear* (Puffin)

Yolen, Jane, *Dragon's Blood; Heart's Blood* (Julia Macrae)

Zindel, Paul, *The Pigman* (Bodley Head)

Poetry   Foster, John, *The 3rd, 4th and 5th Poetry Books* (Oxford)

Hughes, Ted, *Season's Songs* (Faber)

Lewis, Naomi, *Messages* (Puffin)

McGough, Roger, *Sky in the Pie* (Kestrel)*; The Kingfisher Book of Comic Verse* (Kingfisher)

McGough, Roger and Rosen, Michael, *You Tell Me* (Kestrel)

Nash, Ogden, *Custard and Company* (Viking Kestrel)

Rosen, Michael, *Wouldn't You Like To Know* (Puffin)*; The Kingfisher Book of Children's Poetry* (Kingfisher)

Styles, Morag, *I Like That Stuff; You'll Love That Stuff* (Cambridge)

Waters, Fiona, *Golden Apples* (Heinemann)

Woodward, Zenka and Ian, *Witches' Brew* (Hutchinson)

Wright, Kit, *Poems for Over Ten Year Olds* (Kestrel)

Books for parents

Babies Need Books (Penguin)*; Five to Eight* (Bodley Head) by Dorothy Butler

Learning to Read by Margaret Meek (Bodley Head)

The Read Aloud Handbook by Jim Trelease (Penguin)

Reading and Loving by Leila Berg (Routledge & Kegan Paul)

Parent, Teacher, Child by Alex Griffith and Dorothy Hamilton (Methuen)

Book Talk by Aidan Chambers (Bodley Head)

The Good Book Guide to Children's Books (published annually) edited by Bing

Taylor & Peter Braithwaite (Penguin)
Puffins for Parents by M. Robinson (Penguin)

Australia	*The PETA Guide to Children's Literature* edited by Walter McVitty (Primary English Teaching Association) *Helping Your Child to Read – A Guide for Parents* edited by Diane Snowball (Nelson) *Reading Begins at Home* by Dorothy Butler and Marie Clay (Victoria: Primary Education) *Helping Your Child With Reading* (Education Department of South Australia) *Magpies – Talking About Books for Children* (5 issues a year; c/o The Singing Tree, 10 Armagh St, Victoria Park, Western Australia 6100) *Reading Time* (4 issues a year; published by The Children's Book Council, P.O. Box 159, Curtin A.C.T. 2605)
England	*Signal: Approaches to Children's Books* edited by Aidan Chambers (3 issues a year; The Thimble Press, Lockwood, Station Road, South Woodchester, Glos., GL5 SEQ) *Growing Point* (6 issues a year; published by Margery Fisher, Ashton Manor, Northampton, NN7 2JL England)
United States	*The Horn Book* (6 issues a year; Circulation Dept., Horn Book Inc., Park Square Building, 31 St James Ave, Boston, Mass. 02116 U.S.A.)